The Fabian Society

The Fabian Society is Britain's leading political society, committed to creating the political ideas and policy debates which can shape the future of progressive politics.

With over 300 Fabian MPs, MEPs, peers, MSPs and AMs, the Society plays an unparalleled role in linking the ability to influence policy debates at the highest level with vigorous grassroots debate among our growing membership of over 7000 people, 70 local branches meeting regularly throughout Britain and a vibrant Young Fabian section organising its own activities. Fabian publications, events and ideas therefore reach and influence a wider audience than those of any comparable think tank. The Society is unique among think tanks in being a thriving, democratically-constituted membership organisation, affiliated to the Labour Party but organisationally and editorially independent.

For over 120 years Fabians have been central to every important renewal and revision of left of centre thinking. The Fabian commitment to open and participatory debate is as important today as ever before as we explore the ideas, politics and policies which will define the next generation of progressive politics in Britain, Europe and around the world.

Find out more at **www.fabians.org.uk**

Fabian Society
11 Dartmouth Street
London SW1H 9BN
www.fabian-society.org.uk

First published April 2006

ISBN 0 7163 4102 6

This report, like all publications of the Fabian Society, represents not the collective views of the Society but only the views of the authors. This publication may not be reproduced without express permission of the Fabian Society.

British Library Cataloguing in Publication data.
A catalogue record for this book is available from the British Library.

Printed by Bell & Bain, Glasgow
Cover photo by Third Avenue
Editorial Director: Tom Hampson

Narrowing the Gap

The final report of the Fabian Commission on
Life Chances and Child Poverty

Contents

Part Three: Closing the gap in life chances

Preface

As the Chief Executive of Turning Point, I am privileged to lead an organisation that makes a real and often rapid difference to the lives of thousands of people with complex needs, including those affected by drug and alcohol misuse and mental health problems. As a social care organisation, we are the largest provider of Progress to Work services in the country and amongst the largest providers of services to people with learning difficulties.

I agreed to chair the Fabian Commission on Life Chances and Child Poverty because it was established to address – in a very different way to Turning Point – many of the same issues of deep and persistent disadvantage in our affluent society. As well as making specific policy recommendations, the Commission hopes to change the way these debates are conducted, by putting equal life chances at the heart of our vision of the good society and our thinking about how to get there.

There can be no doubt whatsoever that poverty and inequality are major problems in the UK today. At present around one in five British children is living in poverty. This blights both their experience of childhood and their chances of being healthy, living safely, and developing successfully into adulthood. This poverty and disadvantage is concentrated in specific social and ethnic groups. As well as offending against out basis sense of justice, everyone in society has reason to be concerned about the economic and other costs of failing to address this situation.

Our society does not have to be like this. To paraphrase the Prime Minister, we can be the generation to abolish poverty in the UK. We can also be the generation to begin narrowing the dramatic inequalities in life chances experienced by different children. Yet these ambitions demand clarity about what we are trying to achieve, and a huge investment of political capital. The Fabian Commission has developed a philosophical approach and a language that is designed to meet this challenge.

We believe that the life chances approach can be used to build a wide coalition for progressive policies. Whilst only a minority of people live in poverty, everyone wants better life chances. The life chances approach recognises the importance of opportunities and risks, and tells a realistic story about why some people are so much less likely to succeed than others. It then asks three questions of each area of public policy: what does this do for life chances; what does it do for the life chances of the most disadvantaged; and is it likely to narrow the gap in life chances between the most disadvantaged and the rest?

Using this framework we have made a number of key recommendations in relation to welfare reform and public services, which are set out in the summary and body of this report. The story in outline is this: income matters, and welfare benefits and tax credits matter a lot for those living in poverty. Income support rates for pregnant women should be a particular focus for future increases in spending, as should Child Benefit rates. On public services the government needs to hold its nerve and keep increasing investment in early years services; extend its focus into the period before birth when some of the most dangerous risks occur for children; and start seriously to address inequality in educational outcomes at school. Poverty and unequal life chances need to move to the centre of the government's agenda, and in particular to the centre of the Chancellor's 2007 Comprehensive Spending Review.

The Commission is extremely grateful for the generous financial support it received through grants from the Barrow Cadbury Trust, the Sutton Trust, the Webb Memorial Trust, and the Dartmouth Street Trust. The Commission would like to thank the Barrow Cadbury Trust for its generous support for the original project, as well as its funding of the deliberative research commissioned from MORI. Particular thanks are due to Sukhvinder Stubbs, who has been closely involved with the project from the outset, to Shazia Awan, for her help in contacting several of the grassroots organisations for the qualitative research, and to Phoebe Griffiths, especially for her astute and insightful comments on the text. The Commission has met regularly since its launch in March 2004, and the members of the Commission are very grateful to the Royal Bank of Scotland for providing the facilities for its meetings.

The Commission's work has been led by Louise Bamfield and Richard Brooks, Research Fellow and Research Director respectively at the Fabian Society. The research for the Commission has primarily been undertaken by Louise Bamfield, of the Fabian Society, and Sadia Haider, who conducted the data and statistical analysis for the project until March 2005. Additional research assistance was provided by Sophie Moulin, Barney Gough, and James Parker. The Commission would also like to thank various other members of the Fabian staff including: Sunder Katwala, for leading the public dissemination strategy for the Commission; Tom Hampson and Jonathan Heawood, for setting and copy editing the texts of the final report and interim report respectively; Giles Wright, for proofreading the final text; Margaret McGillen and Claire Willgress for their administrative support; and the events team of Emma Burnell, Jessica Studdert, Jamie Hodge and Lorriann Robinson for all their help in organising the Life Chances Lecture Series in spring 2005 and other Life Chances events.

This report has been written by Louise Bamfield and Richard Brooks under the direction of the Commissioners. Particular thanks are due to Fran Bennett and Ruth Lister for their very thorough reading of each draft and for their many valuable suggested amendments and revisions.

Lord Victor Adebowale
Chair, Fabian Commission on Life Chances and Child Poverty
April 2006

Summary

The life chances framework

1 This Commission addresses three main **challenges**. First, despite recent progress, one in five children in the UK still lives in poverty. Second, chances in life remain very unequal for children from different backgrounds, and in many cases the gaps are not closing. Third, despite their underlying support for progressive policies, the public does not currently give high priority to tackling poverty and inequality.

2 We believe that the concept of **life chances** should be central to a new politics of equality. It works on three levels. First, we believe it can clarify what are often confused philosophical debates about equality by explaining which inequalities matter and why, and by cutting through debates about equality of opportunity versus equality of outcome. Second, it offers a litmus test with which to assess policy options by asking how far they improve life chances and narrow inequalities, and has the potential to provide a coherent strategy to underpin policy across health, education, the labour market and other key areas. Third, it enables government to 'go public' with a compelling vision and public narrative of why it wants to eradicate child poverty, which is essential to win support for a more equal society and embed it at the heart of a new progressive consensus.

3 Children born in different circumstances in the UK today have very different chances of enjoying good health, a good

level of personal development and education, and a safe environment in which to live – outcomes which can have knock-on effects through later life. Perhaps most fundamentally, not every child is given the chance to flourish and to enjoy a secure and happy childhood. The concept of life chances helps us focus on the risks faced by children from different backgrounds. In particular low income, low socio-economic status, disability, and membership of particular ethnic groups are associated with much higher risks. Many children will 'make it' despite coming from a disadvantaged background. However, on average these social groups experience **systematically worse outcomes**. We believe this offends against fundamental principles of fairness.

4   **Poverty** is the inability, due to lack of resources, to participate in society and to enjoy a standard of living consistent with human dignity and social decency. Growing up in poverty has a particularly serious impact on children's life chances, so ending child poverty will be a central part of improving the life chance of disadvantaged children. We strongly support the government's objective of ending child poverty in the UK by 2020, recognise the progress that has been made in recent years in reducing child poverty, and believe that our recommendations would help to achieve the long term goal.

5   Part Two of this report investigates some of the many ways in which poverty and other disadvantages affect life chances. It is of particular concern that despite significant progress in relation to both child poverty and standards in public services, in many cases the **gap in life chances** between disadvantaged children and their peers has failed to narrow significantly since 1997. For example:[1]

   • The infant mortality rate among children whose parents were in routine or semi routine occupations was double that for the children of managers and professionals in 2000-02. This gap has widened since 1994-96.

- In 2002 children with parents in routine occupations were less than half as likely to achieve at least five GCSEs at A*-C grade as children with professional parents, and there were also big gaps in results between different ethnic groups. The gap in average points score at the end of Key Stage Two between pupils who receive free school meals and their peers has not narrowed since 1998.

- 21 per cent of all children in Great Britain lived in poverty in 2003/04, down from 25 per cent in 1996/97.[2] However, the poverty rate among children of Pakistani and Bangladeshi origin was three times as high at 61 per cent.

6   We believe that politicians, policy makers and those responsible for public services should now put life chances at the centre of what they do. Policies should be tested against the questions: 'What does this do for life chances? What does it do for those who currently have the worst chances in life? Does it narrow the gap or widen inequalities in life chances?' Government in particular should start to measure, report on and **target the gaps in life chances**.

Recommendations

7   The **recommendations** that flow from our work attempt to improve life chances for disadvantaged children and close the gap between them and their more fortunate peers. They are set out in Part Three of this report and the summary conclusions are reproduced below.

8   We are also telling a story about support for children from before birth to the end of school and beyond: government must hold its nerve on the early years agenda, extend its focus to the period before birth, and start to address unequal chances at school. In this story, **public services and income both matter** for life chances, as do a complex web of other factors that affect children and families. Direct financial sup-

port for those on low incomes will remain very important, and increases in benefit rates for pregnant women are a key priority.

9 ▶ **Recommendation 1**

The government's child poverty commitments must be identified as a central national priority in framing the 2007 Comprehensive Spending Review, reaffirming the commitment to halving child poverty by 2010 relative to its 1999 baseline and eradicating it by 2020. The government should, during 2006, conduct a cross-cutting and cross-departmental **Review of Life Chances in the UK***, and of the government activity necessary to narrow gaps in life chances.*

10 ▶ **Recommendation 2**

The government should institute a regular **annual Life Chances Audit** *which details progress on improving and equalising life chances for children and young people in the UK. It would bring together evidence on all the main strands of work across government that address inequalities in life chances, and would inform media and public debate about the key facts and trends in inequalities in the UK.*

11 ▶ **Recommendation 3**

The current pattern of **maternity support** *should be refocused so that it is more concentrated on disadvantaged mothers whose children suffer the worst outcomes, especially in terms of low birth weight and infant mortality. This additional support should be better linked to wider early years' services such as high quality childcare as well as parenting support programmes.*

12 ▶ **Recommendation 4**

There should be a statutory right to a year's **paid parental leave** *which is transferable between parents, including an element of 'use it or lose it' leave reserved for fathers. This would help low-income parents take up their leave entitlements and encourage fathers to accept greater parental responsibilities.*

13 ▶ **Recommendation 5**

*The UK should aspire to a system of **universal high quality childcare**, with government playing a role in both subsidising parental demand for childcare and in directly supporting the supply of places. However, public spending should be re-balanced from subsidising demand through tax credits, towards directly supporting the supply of high quality places. This would reduce costs for parents and provide a powerful mechanism for improving standards in the childcare sector.*

14 ▶ **Recommendation 6**

*For the 2007 Comprehensive Spending Review, the government should develop Public Service Agreement targets to **reduce inequalities in educational attainment** between disadvantaged groups and their peers from Foundation Stage onwards. These targets could be expressed in similar terms to those that already exist in relation to health outcomes and employment rates among disadvantaged groups.*

15 ▶ **Recommendation 7**

*Education policy should narrow inequalities in life chances and ensure it does not exacerbate them. **Admissions policies** should be reviewed to reduce segregation by socio-economic background across the schools system. **Education funding** needs to follow need more strongly, and the **schools audit and inspection system** should develop a clearer focus on narrowing inequalities in educational outcomes between pupils from disadvantaged backgrounds and their peers.*

16 ▶ **Recommendation 8**

*As a first step towards additional direct financial support, a **'pregnancy premium' to income support** should be introduced for pregnant women. This would help address poverty among pregnant women and would promote the health of babies at the very start of life when they are most vulnerable.*

17 ▶ **Recommendation 9**

*Overall **benefit rates for children** should increase at least in line with average earnings or faster, so that their standard of living rises and more children are lifted out of poverty. Universal Child Benefit and means-tested Child Tax Credit should remain the twin foundations of this approach, but the system should be re-balanced to give a greater role for **Child Benefit**. This would allow both elements to work more effectively alongside each other. One option would be to increase the rate of Child Benefit for second and subsequent children over the medium term so that it is closer to the rate for the first child.*

18 ▶ **Recommendation 10**

*We endorse the priority that the government has given to improving the level of direct financial support for children. However, the present low level of **financial support for adults with and without children not in paid work** threatens to militate against the effectiveness of other policies directed at improving children's life chances. Levels of financial support for this group should therefore be increased to adequacy level as measured by minimum income standards. This would help protect today's children and those yet to be born from the effects of poverty as well as recognise the needs of adults living on benefit.*

19 ▶ **Recommendation 11**

*Many children live in poverty despite one or both parents doing paid work. The **minimum wage** should be increased relative to average earnings as rapidly as is compatible with continued increases in employment rates for groups with currently low employment rates (including certain ethnic minorities, disabled people and lone parents), and with continued economic stability and growth.*

20 ▶ **Recommendation 12**

*The UK **tax system** currently takes a similar share of income across the income distribution, and should become more progressive. We support the recommendations of the previous Fabian Commission on Taxation and Citizenship for the introduction of* *a new higher rate of income tax for top earners, and a reform of inheritance tax to shift the burden of such taxation from the estate of the deceased to the recipients of bequests.*

21 ▶ **Recommendation 13**

*We believe that the government should set a target to reduce **income and wealth inequalities** over time where these affect life chances, and should develop and then give prominence to monitoring appropriate indicators of income and wealth inequality.*

22 ▶ **Recommendation 14**

*The government should convene a **Royal Commission on the Distribution of Income and Wealth**, whose remit should include reviewing the impact of existing patterns of remuneration and wealth on children's life chances, engaging the public with its deliberations and making proposals focused on improving the life chances of disadvantaged children.*

23 In addition, we strongly support a number of **existing government objectives** including: the reduction of teenage pregnancy rates; the reduction of health inequalities including in relation to infant mortality and life expectancy; the reduction of the number of young people aged 16-17 who are not in employment, education or training; and improvement in the employment rates of disadvantaged groups so as to close the gap with the overall employment rate.

24 We also urge the government to do more to address inequalities in children's experience of school, to ensure that no child is prevented from participating fully in school life due to lack of resources. Ensuring an inclusive school experience for all children is tremendously important, not least because the impact on children's attitudes towards their peers in poverty could be the foundation of public attitudes towards people in poverty when they grow up.

Politics and public opinion

25 Ending child poverty and improving life chances is a project for the long term. However, it requires a major **injection of political will and energy** now. Public support for the policies necessary to achieve our objectives cannot currently be relied upon. But both government and the broader progressive movement can and must build on those elements of public opinion that are sympathetic.

26 Large majorities of the public think that the gap between high and low incomes is too big, and the latest evidence from the British Social Attitudes Survey shows that there is broad underlying support for a redistributive system of taxation, welfare benefits and public services. Our own research indicates that people think poverty in the UK is unnecessary and wasteful, and once they know about the 2020 target they are supportive. The government's uncompromising objective to **end child poverty at home** is particularly clear and powerful and has the potential to mobilise mass public support. People intuitively understand the way that families are vital for children's life chances, and also understand how better off parents are better able to support their own children.

27 On the other hand we also know that the public accords relatively low priority to the issue of child poverty, and that they are less confident about the state's role in reducing inequality than they are about the injustice of the current situation. Our own research suggests that non-poor people can hold powerful negative stereotypes of the 'undeserving poor', have difficulty with the concept of relative poverty in an affluent society, and have little understanding of the way in which poverty affects life chances. We thus need a **revolution in empathy** if there is to be secure long-term support for our programme.

28 The life chances framework has a key role to play in developing such empathy and a progressive **political narrative**. It

fits with people's intuitive understanding that life is not pre-determined by socio-economic position, and that people do have choices, whilst drawing attention to the fact that some people face greater risks and more limited opportunities. It should help us to develop the realistic narratives about poverty that are necessary to counter existing stereotypes of 'beer and fags and scratch-cards'.

29 The life chances approach can also build a **wider coalition** of support for progressive policies than a focus on poverty alone. If progress towards the 2020 goal is to be sustained, it is essential, for both moral and strategic reasons, that we motivate a broader group of the population for the cause of better life chances for all. Furthermore, although our focus in this report has been domestic, we believe that the life chances framework should also form part of a consistent and princi-pled approach to economic and social rights at the interna-tional level, which would tackle poverty in both industrialised and developing countries in a co-ordinated way.

30 We reject the idea that politics is now simply about who can manage the economy and public services most effectively. The life chances agenda should be central to the battle between competing visions of the good society. It presents the opportunity for Labour to renew its claim to be the party of social justice by showing it has a distinctive, progressive political mission. It also offers the credibility test for a Conservative Party which has declared its ambition to move to the centre ground and to test all of its policies by their impact on the worst off. A genuinely **progressive consensus** needs to put ending child poverty and improving and equal-ising life chances together at its heart.

31 Equalising life chances and ending child poverty should sit together at the heart of a progressive vision of what makes a fair society in which all can flourish. We believe that this vision can have real public appeal. It is a challenge to us all:

to improve children's life chances, to narrow the gap in life chances, and to make poverty history at home.

Notes

1   See Part Two for a detailed presentation including sources.

2   These figures are for 2003/04, based on a relative poverty measure, 60 per cent of median equivalised contemporary household income before housing costs (BHC). Using a measure of relative poverty *after* housing costs (AFC), 28 per cent of all children in Great Britain lived in poverty in 2003/04, down from 33 per cent in 1996/97 (see Table 2.6.2.2 in section 2.6.2).

Part One:
Politics, principles and public opinion

Introduction

What is this report about?

This is the final report of the Fabian Commission on Life Chances and Child Poverty. It focuses on two inter-related but distinct issues: low income and lack of resources among families with children, and the differences in life chances faced by children from different backgrounds. This first section sets out briefly what we are concerned about, what the report is intended to achieve and who it is for, why we think the issues it addresses are important now, and how the report is structured.

For a child to be living in poverty means that they are unable to enjoy the kind of childhood taken for granted in the wider society because their parents lack the necessary material resources to provide them with a decent standard of life. We expand on what we mean by poverty in section 1.3. However, it is not our intention to discuss measures of poverty or the meaning of a 'decent standard of life' used in our definition in this report as these have been well rehearsed elsewhere. Instead, our focus will be on how to address the problem, and in particular how to build deeper and broader public support for the project of ending child poverty. As part of this, we will have a lot to say about the way in which child poverty is understood by the UK public.

By contrast the idea of children's life chances may be relatively unfamiliar, though its basic premise is easy to grasp. At its heart is the simple recognition that children born in different circumstances in Britain today face very different chances of enjoying desirable outcomes such as good health, a good level of personal development and education, or a safe environment in which to live. Perhaps most fundamentally, not every child is given the chance to flourish and to enjoy a secure and happy childhood. Children's chances in life are affected by factors such as their family background, ethnicity and income, whether or not they have a disability, and where they are born in the UK. Their life chances are also affected by government policies, as well as by luck. We believe that the concept of life chances has great potential as a way of thinking about some of the most important political and social issues that face us today. In particular, we will try to make the case that life chances should be fundamental to progressive politics, and at the heart of a new egalitarian political project. It is for this reason that the report is titled 'Life Chances – the new politics of equality'.

What is it intended to achieve and who is it for?

One of the key purposes of the Commission and this report is thus to raise the profile of the concept of life chances, and to establish it as an important tool for achieving political change. We believe that life chances should become central to the way that progressive people and organisations, including political parties and the government, think about tackling inequality and disadvantage. In this context the life chances framework is a way of helping individuals and organisations answer the question 'what are we trying to achieve?' This has particular importance for the Labour Party and the Labour government, now in the process of renewing itself after two full terms in office. When progressive organisations ask themselves what they are for, we argue that part of the answer should be 'to close the gap in children's life chances'. This means improving the life chances of disadvantaged children at a faster rate than for children from affluent families so that the gap between children from different backgrounds is reduced.

There is another way in which we want to establish the life chances framework as a practical tool for achieving progressive change, and this is as a political narrative. We do not make the claim that the words 'life chances' themselves have any particular purchase on the public imagination. Rather, we will try to set out why the life chances approach is politically and philosophically compelling, and will set this in the context of some very significant challenges in terms of public opinion towards poverty and inequality. Our claims here are that more equal life chances can be an inclusive agenda with broad political appeal, which raises issues not only about the most deprived children, but also about inequalities in life chances across the social spectrum; that it enables us to give political coherence to what can be a confusing set of policy agendas; and that it provides a way forward out of stale debates about equality of opportunity versus equality of outcomes.

Another central purpose of the Commission and this report is to support the government's objective of abolishing child poverty in the UK by 2020. This is perhaps the most ambitious and impressive of all Labour's domestic ambitions. However, in addition to the leadership given by the government, we do not believe that it can be achieved without a significant increase in the degree to which the public understands the nature and effects of child poverty in the UK, and agrees with the urgency of addressing the problem. Those who are serious about abolishing child poverty face very significant challenges in terms of public attitudes. This report tries to recognise and understand those challenges, and then find a way of responding to them.

We hope that the ideas and argument of this report will be of interest to a broad politically engaged readership, and as a result it is written in a way that is meant to be fully accessible for a non-technical and non-specialist audience. A key audience for this report is those people who make or influence political decisions from local to national level, and for these we hope the political arguments will be particularly useful. In addition, we hope that the report and the life chances framework in particular will be useful to a wide range of practitioners who are involved with the delivery of public services, whether they are working in the public, private or third sectors.

Why are we writing it now?

Perhaps the most striking thing about child poverty as a political issue is the relatively low profile it has in our national political debates. Not only is the problem severe and widespread, not only is it expensive and difficult to address, but in addition the government has made a clear commitment to abolishing it on a stated timetable. In any other area of policy, this would be likely to generate the most intense scrutiny and debate. Yet even in the past three general election campaigns child poverty has hardly featured as a topic for discussion.

In 1999, the government adopted the objective of abolishing child poverty in 20 years, setting interim targets of achieving a quarter reduction by 2005 and halving child poverty by 2010. The current evidence suggests that the government will come close to reaching its first interim target.[1] But despite the welcome progress so far, around 2.6 million children still lived in families with incomes below the poverty line in 2003/04.[2] This is equivalent to just over one in five children in the UK, a very high rate by European standards.

The early success in tackling child poverty has stemmed principally from two factors. One has been increasing employment rates among low- income families. The other has been increasing financial support for low- income families in the form of benefits and tax credits. This is a tremendously positive story, to be set alongside economic stability, overall employment growth, rising average household incomes and improvements in public services. However, UK employment rates are now near their all time high, and it is likely to become more difficult to sustain the rate of progress in this area. Meanwhile, the UK fiscal environment is tightening in a way that means spending on child poverty will have to compete more vigorously with other priorities. In effect, the government has been able to address child poverty without having to expend large amounts of public political capital. This is unlikely to be the case in the relatively near future, and extremely unlikely to be the case consistently over the coming 15 years. We thus believe that child poverty cannot be eradicated without both renewed policy focus and deeper, broader public support than exists at the moment. This makes it important now to build a coalition to eliminate UK poverty on a similar scale to that mobilised by Make Poverty History in relation to global poverty.

It is more difficult to summarise what has happened to children's life chances in recent years, because there are many different aspects to this question. In this report we focus on children's chances of achieving good outcomes, both in childhood and adulthood, in terms of their health, education and income and other outcomes, including their security, physical environment, and social networks. In many respects, life chances for children have improved on average, both in recent years and over the longer term. However, children from more affluent or fortunate backgrounds still have much better chances than children from disadvantaged backgrounds. In addition, children from more affluent or fortunate backgrounds have generally seen their outcomes improve *as much as or more* than children from disadvantaged backgrounds. For example, school children who are entitled to free school meals do less well on average in examinations, and they have failed to catch up with their peers in recent years. Children born to parents in manual occupations have lower life expectancy than children born to professional parents, and the gap appears to be widening rather than closing.

As well as focusing attention on *class* differentials, the life chances agenda also draws attention to disparities amongst children from different ethnic backgrounds. Importantly, the picture here is far from homogeneous, and we need to recognise the complex pattern of outcomes between and within minority ethnic groups: for example, while many minority communities now achieve above average results in education and are statistically over-represented in higher education, a clear 'ethnic penalty' in employment and income remains, with some minority groups or subgroups among the most marginal and disadvantaged in Britain.[3,4] The life chances agenda provides a compelling narrative for focusing on the most disadvantaged groups from all ethnic backgrounds (including white people), and for tackling discrimination and prejudice in all its forms. This means tackling persistent racial discrimination, as well as prejudice against Muslim people that has emerged more recently. It also means being aware of the humiliating and stigmatising effects of *poverty*, which occurs when people on very low incomes are treated insensitively or without respect.[5] The government has taken a positive lead on challenging discriminatory attitudes against women, ethnic minorities, disabled people and other marginalised groups, which we welcome. But we urge it to apply similar energy and leadership to change public opinion by challenging stereotypical views of people living in poverty.

As with the case of poverty, we feel that it is important to increase the public profile of these issues, and to increase the level of public understanding and support for action now. We believe that an important part of this will be developing a clear story about which sorts of inequalities matter and why, as this has been relatively absent from public debate. Many of the most fundamental inequalities in life chances, such as those reflected in unequal life expectancy and child development, are the product of very complex processes that are hard for public policy to address in isolation. Without solid public support the long term policies necessary to address unequal life chances are unlikely to be sustainable.

In making the case for more equal life chances, we seek to build upon an emerging shift in policy and political thinking, which we welcome. Even in the last six months, there have been signs of a potentially significant shift towards acknowledging the argument that an explicit commitment to tackling inequality as well as poverty is essential. This argument was central to our interim report, which was critical about the failure of government to make its mind up about this central issue, and is expanded upon and developed in this report. It is important to emphasise the scale of the task: rather than a simple continuation of existing policies, what is needed is a major shift in priorities, as part of a long-term political project. Government can only hope to achieve a society in which people's life chances are more equal through an open, public, political strategy.

How has the Commission gone about its work?

A significant part of this report is taken up with setting out the evidence of poor life chances for children from disadvantaged backgrounds, investigating the reasons behind these, and making recommendations to address them. Whilst we provide a broad overview of poverty and inequality in the UK, we do not attempt to provide a comprehensive audit, so the report is not primarily intended as a reference work for this purpose.[6]

Nonetheless it should make a useful introduction for many people to some of the key facts and arguments relevant to this area of public policy.

Many of the empirical questions that we touch on, for example the precise relationship between family income and child outcomes, or the precise effects of formal childcare, are the subject of ongoing investigation and current disagreement. This report does not publish any new quantitative empirical work, but draws instead on a growing body of knowledge pertaining to children's unequal life chances. This analysis allows us to make some key recommendations for public policy. In some cases our recommendations relate to objectives rather than to specific mechanisms to achieve them. In other areas we feel there is sufficiently strong evidence to make more specific proposals, and in these cases the real obstacle to action is often a political one rather than the lack of knowledge.

Since the launch of the Commission in March 2004, its work has been guided by regular meetings of Commissioners, which have been held approximately every two months and have been serviced by staff at the Fabian Society. The work of the Commission has also been informed by the findings of small-scale qualitative research, which allowed us to gain an understanding of the views of two important groups of people. First, as set out in our interim report, the Commission recognised the importance of investigating the views and attitudes of people not living in poverty themselves towards children and families in poverty.[7] In order to explore how the public understands poverty and disadvantage, the Commission engaged MORI to carry out some original deliberative research in early 2005. The participants were drawn broadly from the middle of the political spectrum, from socio-economic classes BC1C2, and from London and the South East of England. While this kind of small-scale, in-depth work does not provide a statistically robust survey of the state of public opinion, it offers insight into the possible causes of attitudes and ways we may be able to change them. In section 1.4, we summarise the findings of the deliberative research, before investigating in more detail their implications for how to develop a political strategy that will build public support for ending child poverty and improving the life chances of disadvantaged children.

Second, in recognition of the importance of learning from people with experience of poverty, we conducted a number of grassroots focus group interviews in London and the West Midlands in summer 2005.[8] The focus groups explored a range of issues and problems encountered by people in poverty as the 'endusers' of public services, as well as examining the role of local community groups and organisations in helping them to overcome the problems associated with life in poverty. Where appropriate, in Part Two of this report we draw upon the findings of this research to illustrate our analysis.

How is the report structured?

Sections 1.2 to 1.4 of this report set out the political and philosophical context for the challenge of addressing child poverty and unequal life chances. In section 1.2 we discuss the inheritance of the 1997 Labour government, the development of the government's social policy objectives, and the public arguments that have accompanied these. This leads us to a statement of our objectives and a discussion of the principles behind these, where we set out our case for making more equal life chances a central objective for policy alongside the eradication of child poverty. We then investigate how the public thinks about poverty and life chances, and what strategies are likely to be most effective in building consent for our objectives.

If the first part of our report sets out what we think should matter and how to make the case for this in principle, Part Two demonstrates that these issues matter in practice, by presenting some of the key facts about child poverty and life chances. The second part also investigates the causes of and relationships between the various aspects of disadvantage so as to inform the policy conclusions reported in Part Three. A conclusion draws out the main proposals and key lines of argument. Throughout the report we attempt to link our political and policy analyses.

UK politics

In some ways the most important context for this report is still the dramatic growth of poverty and inequality in the UK during the 1980s and early 1990s. During this period the child poverty rate nearly trebled whilst the distribution of household incomes grew dramatically more unequal. We now also know that during this period the association between family background and economic success in later life grew stronger. When Labour came to power in 1997, it inherited a country with the highest level of child poverty in the European Union.[9]

Despite all of this, domestic poverty had played no significant role in Labour's 1997 election campaign, and the party had made no explicit promises to address the issue in its manifesto. Nonetheless, in its first years in office the new government adopted a number of policies that were focused on child poverty, including increases in the generosity of benefits and the introduction of tax credits focused on lower income families. Early in its first term, the Labour government set up a special unit in the Cabinet Office to target action against poverty and social exclusion.[10] Another important and explicit aim of government policy was to increase employment rates, especially among lone parents, and to make work pay via the introduction of a national minimum wage, a reduced starting rate of income tax, and the restructuring of national insurance contributions.[11]

The effect of the government's tax and benefit reforms in its first term of office was generally progressive, with greatest gains in entitlement for the lowest income deciles, and lone parent families and families without wage-earners in particular, and small losses for the highest two income deciles.[12] However, throughout this period the language of government was designed to avoid antagonising a public felt to be sceptical about poverty. 'Rights and responsibilities' and 'work is the best route out of poverty' were the cornerstones of this approach. Successive ministerial speeches emphasised the economic costs of unemployment and welfare spending to society as a whole, with much less attention paid to the intrinsic value of addressing the disadvantage encountered by those in poverty. Where poverty itself was explicitly addressed, the focus was typically on child and pensioner poverty, rather than poverty more broadly. During this period the government can be said to have assuaged public opinion rather than trying to generate or exploit public support for its anti-poverty agenda.

Certainly the clearest public signal of the government's commitment to addressing child poverty was the 1999 pledge to abolish child poverty in the UK by 2020. Yet this remarkable pledge, with its implications of long-term commitment, was given very little prominence in the 2001 election campaign. Labour very successfully fought that election on the twin themes of investment in public services and a strong economy, with headline pledges focused around increases in the number of teachers, doctors, nurses and police recruits. The party neither attempted to make political capital out of what it had already done to address poverty (which meant that by 2001, the UK was no longer languishing at the bottom of the child poverty league table in the EU, as it had been in 1997, but was now fifth from bottom), nor did it try to generate electoral advantage from its continuing commitment in this respect.

But if the government was often reluctant to publicise its own targets on tackling and eradicating child poverty, it was positively averse to addressing explicitly a related issue – that of income inequality, which had fallen far down the political agenda. One episode in the 2001 election campaign illustrates this most clearly: this is the occasion when Tony Blair was unwilling to answer Jeremy Paxman's question about whether it was acceptable for the gap between the rich and the poor to get wider. His response – in essence that we should worry about the situation of those at the bottom rather than those at the top, that what mattered was poverty rather than inequality – made it clear how sensitive he was about the politics of this issue.

Once again, Labour in government after the 2001 election proceeded to implement policies which were designed to reduce income poverty. In the 2002 Budget, Gordon Brown announced the creation of two new tax credits from April 2003: the Child Tax Credit and the Working Tax Credit. These were introduced principally to direct additional financial resources to low-income families with children and to improve the incentives to enter paid employment. They were also intended to be simpler than the various benefits and tax credits that they replaced, and to be less stigmatising, both because part of their value would be received through the wage packet and because around 90 per cent of families with children would be entitled to some Child Tax Credit. The expected impact of the new tax credits was highly progressive, with the biggest gainers in the lowest income deciles.[13]

Another key policy decision, taken at the same time as the introduction of the new tax credits, was to increase rates of National Insurance contributions. The 2002 budget announced a one per cent increase in employee and employer rates, as well as the introduction (in effect) of a new 'top rate' of one per cent above the upper earnings limit for employee contributions. The move was explained at the time as necessary to fund higher levels of NHS spending,[14] and its overall effect was to raise significant additional public resources in a highly progressive manner.

The 2001-05 government's programme of tax and benefits reform was highly progressive. By the time of the 2005 election, the total impact of fiscal reforms since 1997 was estimated to have increased the potential income of the poorest 20 per cent of households by more than 10 per cent, with smaller gains for more than half the population, essentially paid for by still smaller proportionate losses for higher income households.[15]

By the time of the 2005 election, significant progress had been made in reducing the extent of child poverty. We will only know in spring 2006, when the official data become available, whether the government in fact reached its interim target of reducing child poverty by a quarter relative to the 1999 baseline. But the fact that the number of children living in relative poverty had fallen by around 600,000 between 1996/7 and 2003/4 represents a major achievement for a progressive party. But once again, in the election Labour made little at the national level of this success, or its future commitment to the issue, or opposition parties' lack of any similar pledge.

The low profile of poverty in the UK has contrasted sharply in the last year with the high profile enjoyed by Make Poverty History, a campaign for trade justice, more and better aid to poor countries and the cancellation of Third World debt.[16] The Prime Minister and Chancellor of the Exchequer have taken a leading role in persuading the international community to give priority to development aid and extreme poverty. Building on the recommendations of the Africa Commission,[17] the UK government made Africa, together with climate change, the focus of its tenure as chair of the G8 and European Union. Some welcome progress was made on cancelling debt at the G8 summit at Gleneagles in July 2005, which coincided with a series of Live8 concerts and Make Poverty History marches, though the success of the negotiations is contested, and it remains to be seen how much progress is made in practice in actually making global poverty history.

Although the nature of the problems to be addressed in tackling global poverty is rather different, anti-poverty campaigners in the UK have sought to draw lessons from the success of the Make Poverty History campaign in mobilising public support, and have begun to consider what obstacles need to be overcome to achieve a similar high profile for UK poverty issues. Initial reflection suggests that the global poverty campaign provides many valuable lessons for UK anti-poverty campaigners, particularly in terms of learning how to make the political argument and promoting the idea of justice rather than charity; articulating the problem to a wide public audience and the receptivity of that audience, and above all the use of media and coalitions in the development of empathy and understanding and in publicising the progress that has been made.

Given that poverty is increasingly being conceptualised as a denial of human rights,[18] we argue that the links between equalities, human rights and poverty should be a key part of the government's agenda. Since 1997, the UK has taken decisive action on economic and social rights in Europe and the world. The Human Rights Act of 1998, coming into force in 2000, and the UK's signature to the Economic and Social Charter imply greater coordination of anti-poverty measures at home and overseas. Acknowledgment of the influential role of human rights has spread rapidly among campaigning organisations, departments of state and international organisations of every kind. When fully accepted human rights can give additional leverage for action as well as research in the public interest. In 2003, the Joint Committee on Human Rights argued successfully for a strategic, rights-based Commissioner for Children and Young People[19] and also for an integrated Commission for Equality and Human Rights (CEHR) to work in a more concerted way than was proving possible with an assortment of separate bodies against discrimination in all its forms.[20] The broad objective of the CEHR – to integrate action against discrimination and to end the arbitrary separation of types of discrimination and fragmentation of action – is to be welcomed, though the difficulties entailed in achieving this ambitious goal in practice should not be underestimated.[21]

A number of issues relating to the distribution of opportunities and advantages gained prominence over the years of the 2001-05 Parliament. The first of these was a growing realisation that whilst child poverty was falling, income inequality remained high on many measures. Another issue which rose in salience was the question of social mobility. Whilst some of the facts about income inequality and social mobility will be examined in Part Two of this report, both concepts are complex and require some initial discussion here so that we can draw out their political significance.

In discussions of inequality we need to be clear about both whom we are comparing and in what respect we are comparing them. In this report we will examine a range of different inequalities in relation to desirable outcomes such as health status, education and income. In many cases we will then look at the varied experiences of people from different backgrounds, for example when we examine the inequality in average examination results for children with parents from 'higher' and 'lower' social class backgrounds.[22]

'Social mobility' likewise has a number of different interpretations. At its most general, it refers to the process of people moving from one social position to another, where social positions are generally identified by occupational class. Sometimes this movement is considered within generations (e.g. when someone changes occupational category), and sometimes across generations (e.g. when someone moves into a different occupational category from their parents). Social mobility as a concept is closely related to income mobility, which is the process of people moving up or down the income distribution. Finally, social mobility can be considered in absolute terms (what are someone's chances of moving up or down?) and in relative terms (what are their chances of moving up or down relative to someone else's chances, for example someone else who started off in a different place?).

By the end of the 2001-05 Parliament, it was becoming clear that on some key measures, income inequality had not fallen over the course of two Labour governments, despite the highly progressive set of tax and benefit changes that had been introduced.[23] At the same time more and more evidence was coming to light indicating that relative social mobility in the UK had fallen over the closing decades of the 20th century. In particular, a number of studies examined the cohorts of children born in 1958 and 1970, concluding that there was a much stronger association for the latter group between where they started out in life and where they ended up than for those born in 1958, indicating that relative mobility across generations has declined in the last two decades.[24]

Labour in government has remained extremely cautious about engaging with the issues of income inequalities and inequality more generally. By contrast, a number of prominent ministers made speeches prior to the 2005 election that dwelt on the need for government to facilitate greater social mobility. This concern for social mobility should be seen as an important development in Labour's political agenda, insofar as it recognises the powerful influence of parental background on later life outcomes and legitimises government action to address the causes of such inequalities. On the other hand, as we discuss further below, we argue that focusing on mobility is not enough, and may even be unhelpful, since it is liable to encourage concern about the outcomes of the most gifted and aspiring individuals from disadvantaged backgrounds, without attending to the overall distribution of resources and opportunities and without challenging the very existence of an excluding and divisive society.

If tax and benefit reform has been one of the key pillars of Labour's domestic policy agenda since 1997, then another is the process of 'investment and reform' in public services.[25] The issue of children's and young people's services gained prominence in Labour's second term, with the publication in 2003 of the government's green paper, *Every Child Matters* alongside the formal response to the report into the death of Victoria Climbié and the passage of the Children's Act in 2004. Following a wide consultation with people working in children's services, and with parents, children and young people, a national framework for change was launched in November 2004, based on five outcomes identified as key to well-being in childhood and later life: being healthy; staying safe; enjoying and achieving; making a positive contribution; and achieving economic well-being.[26]

Improving the quality of public services for everyone has remained a consistent theme for the Labour government. In part this has been driven by a concern that the most vulnerable members of society rely most on public services and that provision of public services tends to be worst in deprived areas. However, it has also been motivated by the concern that unless their quality is high enough, people who are able to afford private alternatives will opt out, and this would undermine the broad base of political support for the tax funding of public services.

These concerns have translated into big increases in real terms spending on core public services, a wide range of targets for government departments and service providers, and significant structural reforms. From the very outset the government has striven to rebut the accusation that the new spending represents bad value for money. Labour has thus tried to be seen as the critical friend of public services: broadcasting the message that the new expenditure is conditional on improved performance; establishing new audit, accountability and incentive mechanisms; and exerting selective pressure on under-performing providers such as schools, local authorities and hospitals.

The early objectives for this programme of investment and reform were relatively modest, such as smaller class sizes for five, six and seven year olds, and the fast-tracking of young offenders through the criminal justice system. Significant quantities of new money arrived only after the 1998 Comprehensive Spending Review due to the freeze in spending in the first two years of the Labour government. The objectives of the new investment were essentially to drive up average standards, as well as standards at the bottom (known as 'floor' targets) across the public services, focusing on issues of public concern such as hospital waiting times and children's attainment at school.[27]

Part Two of this report examines some of these issues in more detail and attempts to evaluate their outcomes, particularly in relation to disadvantaged groups of service users. The key point to note here is that the central political objectives of the early reforms were to improve average outcomes (and thus satisfy the broad public) and to drive up floor standards (and thus to avoid anyone experiencing unacceptably bad services). Whilst these objectives are of course desirable, they are also perfectly consistent with some groups of the public continuing to experience much better services than others. Floor targets are good for people living in poverty in deprived areas, who often experience the worst public service outcomes. However, they don't target the gap between their experience and that of the more affluent. If outcomes for this latter group are improving faster than outcomes at the bottom, then the gap widens even when things are getting better for the worst off.

Without very much fanfare, and in selected areas only, the government has already started to target inequalities in life chances. The most important area where this is happening is health, where the Department now has a range of targets to narrow existing health inequalities such as the difference in infant mortality rates for different social classes and the difference in life expectancy between those areas with the best and worst outcomes. In 2004 more inequality targets were introduced for the employment rates of disadvantaged groups and for early child development. We think these are very significant political commitments, and believe that there is great scope to build on them as we explain in our policy conclusions in Part Three.

In the run up to the 2005 general election, public service reform rose to the top of the political agenda. The key phrase now used by the government was 'choice and diversity'. Very broadly, diversity has meant a commitment to open up certain areas of public service provision to a range of organisations in the public, private and voluntary sectors, and to separate the functions of commissioning and providing services. Choice is a particularly slippery concept, but has generally been interpreted as the aspiration to enable people to have more control over the public services they use, for example in terms of the location of the hospital where they have an operation.

Both choice and diversity have been the subject of intense political debate. Proponents generally argue that diversity will create incentives for service providers to improve their performance, and that choice will both create such incentives and improve the experience of service users directly (for example because they can be treated at a time and place they prefer). Opponents generally argue that diversity will create wasteful duplication and impair the efficient functioning of existing public providers, and that choice will enable more articulate service users to achieve better outcomes at the expense of others. However, our key argument is not about whether choice and diversity are desirable or undesirable in themselves, but about the objectives of this agenda.

Neither 'choice' nor 'diversity' is a policy, and nor are they objectives in themselves. Rather, they are ideas that can inform policies, and it makes little sense to oppose or support them as bare concepts. On the basis of the evidence provided in Part Two of this report it is clear to us that disadvantaged groups experience systematically poor public services provision. If choice and diversity can be used to improve public services for these groups in a way that improves their life chances and closes the gap with more fortunate service users then we have good reason to support them. However, if the polices based on these ideas improve outcomes for the more affluent and articulate in a way that widens the gap then they should be opposed. At the moment there is insufficient clarity about the objectives of the choice and diversity agenda.

We might add that the kind of choice being offered in recent government proposals – of different schools or hospitals – is a poor substitute for real *autonomy* and control over one's life. As Michael Marmot observes, what characterises being in a low-income and low status position is *lack of control over life circumstances*.[28] In our working lives, for example, we need to consider the level of responsibility and discretion that people in different occupational strata have to make decisions about what to do, and when to do it – not least because jobs with low control put people at higher risk of disease.[29] Similarly, in the domestic sphere, there is evidence that lack of control within the home leads to a higher risk of suffering from depression – something that is 'particularly salient for women', even when they 'work outside the home'.[30] Emphasising autonomy and control in this fuller sense is therefore crucial, because it helps us to recognise the importance of ensuring that everyone has the chance to exercise meaningful choices in all spheres of life.

Furthermore, what is perhaps more important than the weaker form of choice being offered in recent proposals is to ensure that disadvantaged users of public services have a voice in how these services operate and in determining their priorities – and moreover, to promote genuine participation rather than merely superficial consultation of service-users. Much greater emphasis needs to be given to facilitating 'voice', therefore, as well as promoting a fuller, more meaningful interpretation of 'choice'.

*   *   *

For its first two terms, Labour governed with a majority in the House of Commons that was very large by historical standards. The 2005 election returned the party to power with a significantly smaller but still workable majority of 66. Since then, arguments have raged about the correct interpretation of this result, and particularly whether it implies that Labour should shift to the left or right to secure its electoral base. We do not intend to provide our own analysis of the voting at the 2005 election, but we do believe that Labour can secure re-election on the basis of a programme that includes strong commitments on child poverty and life chances, and section 1.4 of this report investigates public opinion in relation to these issues.

Even more recently the political landscape has been changing, with the election of David Cameron as Conservative party leader prompting speculation about the future direction of the Conservative Party. One of the first actions of the new Tory leader was the creation of a social justice commission, which will address the causes and consequences of poverty (amongst other things). The leader has recognised the need to change the party's language and image to appear more inclusive. But a key test of the depth of this commitment to social justice will be whether the Conservatives accept the government's child poverty targets, to abolish child poverty by 2020 and halve it by 2010. A further challenge is posed by our objective of closing the gap in life chances for disadvantaged groups.

Correspondingly, a key challenge for the Labour Party will be to continue differentiating itself as a progressive party against a Conservative opposition. This does not mean 'abandoning the centre ground'. Rather it means being clearer about the values and objectives which underlie its progressive policies, and contrasting these with the values and objectives which underlie the policies and positions of its opponents. Policies themselves do not always communicate values very effectively. One purpose of the life chances framework is precisely to enable progressive organisations to link together the elements of their activities and present them in a coherent way. Another is to illuminate the principles that should inform their policies, and thus help in their formulation as well, and it is to the nature of these principles that we turn in the next section.

The principles of a life chances approach

Before looking more closely at the factors that shape children's life chances, and the impact that poverty has on their prospects, we need to be clear what we mean by these terms, and to explain *why it matters* that such marked differences exist in the life chances of children from different social backgrounds. Although many readers of this report will already agree with the need to address poverty and disadvantage, such clarification is nevertheless important for a number of reasons: first, because poverty and life chances are relatively complex concepts, which can be interpreted in different ways; and second, because we wish to counter a different philosophical approach to disadvantage that focuses exclusively on poverty without giving weight in addition to important inequalities.

As we define it, the concept of 'life chances' refers to the likelihood of a child achieving a range of important outcomes, which occur at successive stages of the life course, from birth and early childhood, to late childhood and adolescence, and into adulthood. The life chances framework is premised on the idea that some kinds of experience and opportunity are fundamental to a person's future prospects. For this reason, we identify a number of dimensions as being particularly important: health and well-being, education, income, occupation, environmental quality, safety and security, social networks, and personal autonomy, all of which, we contend, are essential components of a flourishing life.[31]

Perhaps the most fundamental of all life chances is the chance to live a fulfilling and rewarding life, beginning in childhood. As such, children must be given the chance to enjoy a happy, flourishing childhood and to continue to thrive as they grow up. We therefore reject narrowly instrumental approaches which concentrate exclusively on those outcomes in adulthood that relate to people's productivity as economic agents. What the life chances framework encapsulates, above all, is our vision of the good society as one that provides the necessary resources for all its members to live a full and flourishing live and to fulfil their various roles, including as parents, siblings, friends, employees and employers, and citizens.

We should also make it clear that our primary focus is on the relative life chances of people from different social groups. The fact that two children experience different outcomes is not in itself evidence of any injustice, as luck will affect the chances of two individuals differently even where they come from very similar backgrounds. However, luck alone cannot explain why, for example, the average level of qualification is higher amongst the children of richer parents than those whose parents are less well off, or why there are systematic differences in average educational attainment of different ethnic groups. This does not mean that the life chances framework is deterministic, in the sense that background factors such as social class or ethnicity *determine* outcomes in relation to the various dimensions identified above. Some people are able to achieve positive outcomes despite disadvantageous beginnings. But the fact remains that people from certain social groups face higher risks of achieving poor outcomes in later life than their more fortunate peers. These kinds of systematic difference draw attention to a complex set of processes and institutional structures, as well as raising important questions about the justification of those structures.

Not everyone has an equal chance of becoming, say, a Championship footballer or an Ashes-winning cricketer. Nor do we have the same chance of winning Pop Idol, scaling the heights of Mount Everest or of producing prize-winning marrows. Common sense tells us that individuals possess different kinds of talents, abilities and interests, which make them better suited to performing certain kinds of roles or jobs than others. And yet, while many dimensions of diversity enrich human experience. we believe that there is something unjust about the fact that people's chances of enjoying the most fundamental opportunities and necessary outcomes are strongly related to factors outside their control, such as social class, ethnicity or gender.

We object both to the fact that children born into different circumstances have such unequal opportunities and experiences, and the fact that such widely differing rewards and status are attached to the different positions into which people end up in adulthood. For this reason, a life chances approach must address not only unequal opportunities in childhood, but also the underlying structure or distribution of rewards.

At the heart of our approach is the principle of intrinsic equality – the belief in people's equal moral worth, which lies at the heart of democracy and social justice. If we wish to pay more than lip service to the ideal of people's equal moral worth, we need to be able to explain to those who face systematically worse prospects why current social arrangements are – or are not – justifiable.[32] This means tackling the disadvantage and discrimination experienced by those in less advantaged material positions, as well as those who face prejudice on the grounds of their skin colour, ethnic origin, religion, sex, gender or disability. The fact that the current evidence about unequal life chances is so clear provides strong political motivation for redressing these injustices.

1.3.1 The impact of poverty on life chances

Poverty matters because it undermines people's opportunity to flourish and thrive. In other words, it matters because of its effect on their life chances. As we define it, poverty is the inability, due to lack of resources, to participate in society and to enjoy a standard of living consistent with human dignity and social decency. In addition, we define child poverty as the inability to enjoy the kind of childhood taken for granted in the wider society, again due to a lack of resources.

Growing up in poverty affects children's chances across all the dimensions of life chances identified above. Poverty manifests itself not just in forms of material deprivation such as having to go without basic necessities and essential items like a nutritious, balanced diet and decent, safe accommodation. It also manifests itself in the deprivation associated with forms of exclusion from social life, for example being unable to attend after-school clubs or take part in extra-curricular activities. This kind of exclusion – being unable to participate fully in the life of the community – has far-reaching effects on individual health and well-being.[33]

Having to live in poverty is associated with many kinds of negative experience. People on very low incomes are more likely to be treated in disrespectful, belittling or humiliating ways, including sometimes by public sector professionals and service providers. Discrimination of this kind risks undermining children's ability to interact confidently with others and to feel part of a collective entity. This has consequences for their self-esteem and sense of self-worth, which may in turn have repercussions for their physical health. People in poverty are denied the right to self-respect, which has been described as the most basic of all goods.[34]

It follows that poverty is a problem not simply because of the consumer items that people are unable to purchase, but because of its far-reaching impact on the rest of their lives. This can be seen most dramatically, perhaps, in its effect on people's physical health and life span, but also on their ability to access key goods and services and to participate in the life of the wider community. Ultimately, in blighting the lives of children and adults who experience it, in denying people the conditions for respect and social recognition, poverty denies people's basic human rights and so denies the equal moral worth of every citizen.

1.3.2 Does equality matter as well as poverty?

While people at the bottom of the social hierarchy face the bleakest prospects, the gap in life chances also affects people who do not live in poverty. The problems caused by unequal life chances cannot be reduced to an issue dividing the 'haves' from the 'have nots'; rather, it is something that applies across the social spectrum.

To illustrate this, consider the frequently evoked image of two newly born infants lying next to each other in a hospital ward, who are born into widely differing family situations (financially, materially, socially etc.) and thus face widely differing prospects across their entire lives. Despite the power and simplicity of the message, however, it may have the effect of suggesting that the problem predominantly lies with the poor life chances of children from the most disadvantaged backgrounds.

Let us imagine, then, not two, but three infants lying next to each other in a hospital ward, whose parents respectively are high, middle and low earners. What is striking about the comparative prospects of these infants, taking each baby as typical of others in the same income group, is that their average life chances follow a clear pattern: the baby born into the highest income household will tend to have the most favourable chances in life, while those of the baby in the 'middle' position will be less glowing than those of the first infant, but more promising than those of the third baby (whose prospects will, in turn, be bleaker than the other two).

The gap in life chances does not only exist, therefore, between the most disadvantaged, at the bottom, and the rest, but extends across a hierarchy of social positions. As we argue further below, the fact that people have worse chances across the social gradient tells us something fundamental about the fairness of social arrangements.

But how far should our belief in the equal moral worth of every person take us in the direction of other forms of equality? Some critics of egalitarianism claim that what really matters about the distribution of resources is not the fact that people do not have the same chances, but that people at the bottom do not have enough to live a decent life. In other words, we do not just need to demonstrate why poverty matters from a life chances perspective, but also why inequality matters – that is, we need to demonstrate that what matters is not just the position of those at the bottom relative to the middle, but the position of those in the middle relative to the top.

At first glance, the argument from sufficiency may appear persuasive: after all, providing that all have enough, why should we be unduly troubled if some people have more than others? For example, if we look at the wide differences in the quality of housing stock in this country the main problem is that some people do not have access to decent and secure accommodation, not the fact that others at the top of the social hierarchy live in luxury penthouse apartments.

One reason to care about such wider inequalities in society would be if they translated into social divisions which gave rise to problems such as stress, stigma, hostility, violence and prejudice. To a significant degree these are empirical questions: how far do inequalities directly cause other harmful effects? It is therefore extremely timely that the findings of a growing body of epidemiological research on health inequalities should also be pointing us in this direction, providing statistical analysis of the socially corrosive effects of inequality, and helping us to identify the most important dimensions of the social environment for human well-being and the quality of life. In particular, this line of argument has been bolstered by recent studies investigating the psychological and physiological effects of relative inequality on people's health.

Richard Wilkinson and others draw upon a substantial body of evidence to demonstrate that widening income differences in modern societies undermines the quality of social relations. Studies show that increased inequality is linked to declining levels of trust between members of society and declining involvement in community life; increased hostility and homicide rates; and to discrimination against women and ethnic minorities. The empirical evidence underpinning these claims is discussed further in the next chapter. But it is worth highlighting these findings here, because research into health inequalities suggests an important additional set of reasons for attending to the overall distribution of resources and rewards in society.

However, even if inequalities in life chances did not cause other problems in their turn, we should still be concerned about the gradient of inequality and not just the poor outcomes for those at the bottom. The fundamental argument refers back to the principle of equal moral worth. Wherever there is a gradient in life chances, we should be able to explain to the child born in the middle of the distribution why we have chosen social arrangements that result in their chances being worse than those of their more fortunate peers, just as we have to be able to explain to the child at the bottom why their prospects are so bad.

1.3.3 The limits of meritocracy and social mobility[35]

As we see it, there is something fundamentally unfair about the distribution of rewards attached to particular positions in UK society today. For this reason, the life chances framework is necessarily broader than that of social mobility: we are concerned with the chances of everyone living a full and flourishing life, irrespective of how they come to occupy different positions. In other words, even if the processes by which people come to have different outcomes were as fair as possible, taking into account relevant differences between individuals, and ignoring irrelevant differences, there would still be problems with a society which allows its winners to take so many of the prizes.

The concept of meritocracy is similarly problematic from a life chances perspective because it helps to foster the idea that people with higher natural ability are *worth more* than those who do not have the same talents. In monetary terms, of course, it may well be true that those with greater human capital (defined as the capacity to earn income) accrue greater assets, and so are worth more financially; but one's financial assets are a very poor indication of one's moral worth. In this sense, the idea of a meritocracy is liable to become pernicious when the capacity to create wealth is regarded (mistakenly) almost as a type of moral virtue. Wealth-creation is an essential feature of any modern society, but it represents only one type of 'merit'. A broader understanding of the term would give proper social (and economic) recognition to the contribution that people make to the wellbeing of others in society, e.g. by devoting their lives to caring for others, or servicing basic needs in the form of catering and cleaning work. We need to confront the complacent view that a steep hierarchy in social positions is inescapable. As the historical existence of a gender pay gap illustrates, far from being inevitable, hierarchies of rewards can result partly from bias and discrimination in the labour market, and in wider society. Certainly, different occupations are bound to attract variable levels of social and economic reward, but the inequalities in pay and status between jobs on a steeply graded occupational hierarchy are at present artificially large. In particular, given its demonstrated importance for people's health and well-being, more should be done to increase the level of autonomy or control that people are able to exercise over their working lives.

The essential ingredients of living a full and flourishing life, which include autonomy, social recognition, and full social engagement, should not be the preserve of the privileged, but should exist for everyone regardless of their place in the social hierarchy. Although it is difficult to imagine that the gap in people's life chances will ever completely disappear, it is within our power to ensure that the distribution of life chances is more equal. Comparative evidence from studies across and within countries demonstrates that the extent of inequality – the steepness of the gradient – is amenable to change. As we argue in the next section, the momentum for change depends, as ever, on building support for a political agenda which emphasises that the core components of a full and flourishing life should be available to all. But we strongly believe that the moral imperative for social action is undeniable.

Public opinion

Public opinion is of central importance to the project of ending child poverty and addressing unequal life chances in the UK, because without public support, it is unlikely that the government will be able to muster sufficient resources to be able to deal effectively with the problem. The first point to recognise is the scale of the challenge: the public is sceptical about both the need to prioritise poverty and the effectiveness of government action to address it. Furthermore, whilst we know less about their views on life chances, what we do know seems to be at least as challenging. However, the second critical point to recognise is that public opinion can be shaped and led, and that we should not simply accept current attitudes as an absolute constraint on action. This section thus seeks to understand how the public sees poverty and life chances, and begins to develop a strategy of building support for our long-term objectives that involves both working with the grain of public opinion and recognising where and how it is necessary to challenge it.

1.4.1 Quantitative evidence

Broadly speaking, a majority of the British public recognises domestic poverty as an issue, and a large majority thinks that the gap between those on high and low incomes is too wide. However, perceptions of the extent of poverty and its importance appear to have declined significantly over the last decade. In 1994, 71 per cent of people thought there was 'quite a lot' of poverty in Britain, compared to 28 per cent who thought there was 'very little real poverty'. By 2003 the proportion who thought there was quite a lot of real poverty had fallen to 54 per

cent, with an increase in the proportion of those who were sceptical to 41 per cent.[36] Over the course of 1998 between seven and
ten per cent of respondents to MORI's regular poll of 'the most
important issues facing Britain today' cited poverty and inequality as one of their key issues. By 2005 this had fallen slightly to
between five and eight per cent. For comparison, in September
2005 the proportions of people citing crime, education and the
NHS as a key issue were 25 per cent, 21 per cent, and 28 per cent
respectively.[37]

Of course, it is one thing for the public to recognise an issue,
but a different matter for it to think that government has a role
in solving the problem, and another step again to support or
reject specific policies to address the issue. A bare majority currently agrees that the government should 'increase taxes and
spend more on health, education and social benefits'. When
asked about welfare benefits and taxes specifically, support is
slightly lower: in 2003, 43 per cent agreed that 'government
should spend more money on welfare benefits for the poor, even
if it leads to higher taxes'.[38] And yet, in 2000, almost three in four
people agreed with the proposition that it was 'definitely' or
'probably' the responsibility of the government to 'reduce
income differences between poor and rich', against only one in
six who said it is not.[39] Underlying these views may be the explanation that many members of the public support policies whose
effect is redistributive, whilst being wary of policies which call
explicitly for redistribution.[40] Analysis by Tom Sefton of the most
recent findings from the British Social Attitudes Survey reveals
that many people are in favour of redistribution when it occurs
as a 'by-product' of government tax and spending policies, but
are hesitant about the pursuit of redistributive goals for their
own sake.[41] Crucially, we also know that when people are asked
whose taxes should be raised, they appear to have in mind only
the very highest earners – in short, there is general and widespread agreement that it is *other people's taxes* that should go up.

Whilst around 80 per cent of the population agree that 'the gap
between those with high and low incomes is too wide', only
around 40 per cent agree that government should redistribute
income to the less well off.[42] Whilst the proportion who agree

that the gap is too big has been rising over the last decade, the proportion who support income redistribution has been falling, from around 50 per cent in 1994.

Perhaps unsurprisingly, certain groups such as children and elderly people attract much stronger public support for welfare spending, whereas adults without children attract relatively little. In 2003, for example, 66 per cent agreed that the government should top up the incomes of lone parent families on low wages, and 59 per cent agreed that the same should go for couples with children, while only 26 per cent agreed with such support in the case of a couple with no children.[43]

We also know that an increasing proportion of the public is concerned that benefits for the unemployed are too high, and that attitudes in this respect have hardened significantly since Labour came to power. In 2003, 40 per cent agreed that 'benefits for the unemployed are too high and discourage work', compared to 34 per cent who thought that 'benefits for the unemployed are too low and cause hardship'. In the early 1990s, more than 50 per cent of the public supported this latter position, but a big change in public opinion seems to have occurred after 1997.[44] This shift in attitudes may partly reflect events in the public sphere, notably the language used by politicians to discuss adult benefits, as well as changes in the wider socio-economic environment. Certainly, survey data reveal variations over time in people's beliefs about the causes of poverty, with greater sympathy for unemployed people being displayed at times of economic recession. Attitudinal data from the Eurobarometer surveys, for example, shows that British respondents tend to be less convinced by 'laziness' explanations of poverty, and more inclined to attribute poverty to 'unfairness' or 'injustice', at times of economic recession and high unemployment (presumably because they are less likely to regard unemployed people as personally culpable at such times and more likely to know individuals affected).[45] Conversely, higher numbers attribute poverty to 'laziness' or 'lack of will power' at times of economic growth.[46]

We thus have a reasonably informative quantitative picture about attitudes to poverty and income inequality. However, we have very little comparable evidence about public attitudes to the inequalities in life chances that we investigate in this report. This is an important gap in our understanding. In addition, we have relatively little qualitative data that investigates how people understand poverty and why they hold the views that quantitative surveys reveal.[47]

1.4.2 Fabian deliberative work

In thinking about how to develop a political strategy that will build public support for ending child poverty and improving the life chances of disadvantaged children, we draw upon the findings of the deliberative research carried out for the Commission by MORI (see page 7). The results of the deliberative work are extremely challenging for those who share these objectives, but they do not counsel despair. Instead, they indicate some of the practical steps that need to be taken – and which are not being taken at the moment – if we are to sustain progress up to 2020 and beyond.

One of the strongest findings of this work was that our participants had developed their views about poverty and disadvantage principally from sources such as reality television, anecdotal stories and their own experience of growing up. They felt that they had little access to reliable information about these issues in the media or from public sources. They also had very little idea of what government was doing in relation to child poverty; for instance, none of them knew about the goal of abolishing child poverty by 2020.

Their initial concept of child poverty was one of absolute destitution, exemplified by the image of a starving African child. The concept of relative poverty remained difficult for them to grasp even after extensive discussion, and many expressed a degree of bewilderment that real poverty could exist in an affluent society such as ours. When asked to think about child poverty in the UK, many looked for a definition that focused not on financial resources, but rather on the absence of loving and supportive parental relationships. A number cited examples, often from their own experience, of parents who were able to raise their children in a supportive and caring manner despite very limited financial resources. By contrast, the figure of the distant or loveless high-earning parent was evoked as evidence that a child could be 'poor' in an affluent family.

Our participants found it very difficult to empathise with parents living in poverty. One important underlying assumption was that everyone has opportunities and capacities which they are free to capitalise upon if they choose to do so, and that being poor is therefore to some extent a *choice*. 'Opportunity' was a key issue in these discussions, and views about the nature of opportunity in contemporary society were complex and often contradictory. On the one hand, there was the widely held assumption that everyone enjoys opportunities, but it is up to each individual to take advantage of them. On the other hand, evidence that some groups in society do much better than others did not, in the main, elicit any strong reactions. Indeed, when presented with some of the key findings of Leon Feinstein's work on early cognitive development, which shows initially low attaining children from affluent families overtaking high attaining children from low-income families by the age of five,[48] our participants expressed little surprise, and could immediately offer good reasons why more affluent parents could provide advantages for their children.

Our participants thus saw material poverty as being fundamentally about attitudes – a matter of parents not trying hard enough, rather than not having enough. Parents in this situation were easily stereotyped as lazy and wasteful – as spending their time in front of the television and spending what money they have on drugs, alcohol, tobacco and gambling. Several referred to stories from the media about the 'undeserving poor' and offered lurid examples from television shows.

The prevalent view of poverty amongst participants was therefore of poverty as an attitudinal state rather than a material state. This view had two aspects. On the one hand attitudes to work and money were thought to cause material poverty. On the other hand, attitudes to children and parenting were thought to cause the problems associated with child poverty. We believe that these causal stories are critically important in explaining the relatively weak public support for policies to address child poverty.

Our participants also felt that the world had changed in ways that present new challenges to both children and adults. Many were concerned about the stresses and pressures on children both to perform well academically and to fit in socially. Although our discussion focused on poverty, our groups were also concerned by the problems of affluence and excess, exemplified by a culture of greed and consumerism that encroaches into even the early years of a child's life. One response was that if parents lacked the money to buy the latest trainers then this might be no bad thing, and that the children could usefully learn to go without. A number of participants favourably compared their own upbringing with the more consumerist contemporary society. Importantly, however, there was very limited recognition of the ways in which this consumerist environment could generate additional stress for a low-income family, nor how children can be excluded or even bullied if they lack the consumer goods enjoyed by their peers.[49]

1.4.3 Political strategy

In section 1.2 we set out some of the high level political developments since 1997. This presented something of a puzzle: why has Labour taken such progressive policy decisions whilst giving so little prominence to the issues of poverty and disadvantage that these policies are designed to address? In the light of the evidence about public opinion, this approach – to do good by stealth – looks understandable. It is not simply the case that low-income families are a relatively small proportion of the total population, nor that poverty is relatively low down the list of priorities for the general population; it is also the case that the public in fact has deep underlying reservations both about people living in poverty and with the idea of providing the material support that is central to government policy in this area.

When we set the qualitative work alongside the opinion data we cited earlier, we can see a significant political challenge developing. Public support for tackling poverty and disadvantage can currently be characterised as fairly broad but dangerously thin. The quantitative evidence suggests that such support has fallen, and our deliberative work indicates a profound lack of empathy with low-income parents. These attitudes are worrying, given that achieving further reductions in poverty are likely to be at least as challenging as the progress that has already been made. Moreover, as poverty rates fall further, public support for the shrinking group of low-income families may continue to erode. It is therefore becoming urgent to develop a political strategy that improves and in particular deepens the level of public support for progressive policies.

Sefton's recent analysis of public attitudes towards inequality and redistribution highlights a dilemma about whether or not government should pursue an *explicitly* redistributive policy.[50] At first glance, there appear to be high levels of underlying public support for policies that are redistributive in effect – as revealed in people's responses to questions that indirectly addressed redistribution. These findings could embolden the government to pursue a progressive agenda. And yet, there are grounds for caution here too, as many people have reservations about the pursuit of redistributive goals for their own sake.[51] Thus, as Sefton argues, 'an explicitly redistributive agenda would attract the support of a significant minority but may put off many people who might otherwise support these kinds of policies'.[52]

In making the case for a more redistributive agenda, the government needs to tackle popular 'misperceptions about the current system, particularly in relation to taxation', as well as addressing anxieties about fraud and perceived abuse of the system.[53] But simply providing more information about poverty and the relevant government policies is unlikely to be sufficient. In our deliberative work we exposed our discussion groups to just this kind of information, but many participants had difficulty in interpreting the statistical data. In addition, many were highly sceptical of statistical evidence in general, and government statistics in particular. Addressing this kind of lack of trust is well beyond the scope of the Commission, although it is likely to be important to the wider project of progressive government. Most importantly, though, simply publicising an anti-poverty strategy on the basis of the statistics alone will not deal with the underlying issues driving public scepticism.

By contrast, it was only the most direct and illustrative evidence of the effects of poverty and disadvantage that had much effect. Many participants were struck by evidence of material deprivation and severe hardship – such as the proportion of children going without warm coats or three meals a day, while for a few participants evidence of relative poverty, such as not being able to attend birthday parties and not being able to afford to go swimming, had a decisive impact. The latter examples are interesting because they indicate a sense of what people feel is reasonable for a decent childhood, which goes beyond basic clothing. In relation to life chances, evidence about health inequalities was probably the most salient.

Perhaps the strongest and most positive responses were to hearing about the government's pledge to eradicate child poverty and the progress made so far towards reaching its interim targets. There was genuine surprise and encouragement about the figures showing that government policy could make, and had made, a difference. This evidence, showing that child poverty is by no means intractable, was important in countering the often fatalistic view that child poverty is somehow inevitable. Of course, it is important not to overstate the significance of these reactions. Deliberative research occurs in an artificial environment, where the responsiveness of participants is likely to be artificially heightened.

Some aspects of the government's current approach seem to fit well with what we know about public attitudes and understanding, such as the language of 'rights and responsibilities'. Another aspect of the government's approach that seems appropriate is the focus on efficiency in government spending and probity in the administration of welfare benefits. When our deliberative group discussed the potential policy responses to child poverty, many referred to the importance of spending any additional resources well, and we know from opinion surveys that the public generally overestimates the extent of benefit fraud.[54] However, while an approach that stresses 'rights and responsibilities' seems to accord with many people's underlying intuitions and assumptions, it is also important to be aware of the ways in which the language used by government may be reinforcing negative images and stereotypes. Although there are clearly difficulties involved, the government arguably could be playing a much stronger role in leading public opinion than it has done so far, by encouraging greater empathy towards people in poverty.

Our groups were particularly sympathetic to the 'business case' for tackling poverty and disadvantage, which focuses on issues for the rest of society, for example by emphasising the waste of individual potential that poverty and disadvantage represent, the problems they cause such as crime and ill health, and the pressure this generates for palliative public spending. In many ways, this kind of approach would build on an argument that is central to the current government's political strategy, which is that there is no tension between the pursuit of social justice and a strong economy.

More fundamentally, however, we believe that what is needed is a revolution in empathy for people living in poverty and suffering other forms of disadvantage. The primary reason for this is to address the way in which non-poor people understand the causes and consequences of poverty. The objective would not be to evoke sympathy and pity, which the MORI research suggested could serve to distance people still further from the 'other' living in poverty and to increase a sense of helplessness in the face of the problem. Rather, the goal would be to improve understanding of the ways in which poverty and disadvantage actually affect people's lives, and create real barriers to taking up opportunities and achieving positive outcomes.

This means telling stories and developing narratives. Our deliberative work uncovered two powerful narratives which can work against public support for progressive policies. 'Origin stories' provide examples of people who have succeeded against the odds, usually in terms of coming from poor backgrounds yet becoming materially successful. They were often cited by our discussion groups as evidence that poverty does not really limit opportunities. Meanwhile, negative stereotypes provide examples of people whose problems look unrelated to their low incomes, but are rather due to personal faults of laziness and selfishness.

We need to develop a third type of narrative instead that illustrates the real nature of poverty. This could be centred around the 'struggling family', one with agency and opportunities, but facing greater risks and higher barriers because of a lack of resources. Such figures simply do not occur often enough in political discourse, which is dominated by 'hard working families' where the assumption of paid work is central. Similarly, negative stereotypes of non-working people as lazy and feckless are too rarely rebutted by public voices from government or other organisations. We need to counter this kind of stereotype by remembering that the vast majority of low-income parents love their children and want the best for them, just like the vast majority of other parents, but face difficulties in parenting due to lack of resources. This kind of narrative would be supported by evidence that the problem of poverty is not intractable, for example by drawing on data from countries with the lowest child poverty rates, to counter the view that poverty is somehow inevitable.

Whatever the specific narrative device, the purpose must be to improve public understanding of the ecology of poverty: how it develops, what its effects are, how it makes life difficult. Part of this will be about explicitly recognising that not only do some people succeed despite initial disadvantages, but that we should aspire to all people living a 'good life' whatever their background. This must be a story which balances optimism with realism, and respects the autonomy of those experiencing disadvantage without turning it into a reason to leave them to simply fend for themselves.

The basis for this kind of approach already exists in public attitudes. There is a clear recognition that parents are vital to their children's life chances; that all parents and children face risks and pressures in modern Britain; and that more affluent parents have advantages over others in society. What needs to be developed is the understanding of how these risks and challenges can be more problematic for groups such as those with low incomes or low qualifications. This means providing examples and illustrations that show how decisions are made, opportunities can be taken or lost, and problems addressed or passed on.

The concept of life chances is not only important in relation to our objectives, but also has a role to play in this political and communications strategy. We make absolutely no claims for 'life chances' as a catch-phrase. Like many other terms such as 'social exclusion', and 'social mobility' (which our participants thought meant social climbing), it has little or no resonance outside a very small group of people. However, as set out in section 1.3, we argue that the concept of life chances has a number of distinctive strengths as an organising concept, which avoids some of the dangers of social mobility or meritocracy of seeming to favour the advancement of the most talented without addressing the underlying structure of rewards in society.

When we talk about life chances, it becomes clear that we are thinking about disadvantage not in terms of destiny and determinism, but rather in terms of risk. This is both the right factual interpretation of the impact of disadvantage, and it also fits well with public understanding. We found a strong – and well founded – resistance to the idea that a person's background determines their fate. The life chances framework allows us to move past the objection that 'some people make it nonetheless' to a discussion about the obstacles some people really do face in their lives.

It is a continual struggle for government, and many other organisations such as service providers in the public and voluntary sectors, to explain why they are doing what they are doing. For government this is reflected in the problem of policies not cohering into a persuasive political offer. For service providers it can be a problem both for the users and for the employees. The life chances framework can be used both to clarify high level progressive objectives and to facilitate an analysis of the factors that lead to bad outcomes for some groups of people.

The life chances approach also offers a way out of some of the stale debates about equality of opportunity versus equality of outcome, by making it clear that the chance of achieving a good outcome is intimately related to the opportunities faced by people in different circumstances. This in turn strongly depends on the existing structure of rewards (including status and pay) attached to different jobs and positions. It also focuses our minds on which inequalities matter. We discuss some of these in this report, especially those concerned with health, education and child development. It is an ongoing project to consider which outcomes we care about not as means but rather as ends.

This is all particularly important for the political left, for whom equality has long been a motivating principle. However, focusing on life chances enables us to build a broader coalition behind progressive policies. One of the great political advantages of the progressive movement should be the moral force of its arguments. However, the US experience of the recent repeal of inheritance tax provides a powerful cautionary tale that is relevant to the UK. This highly progressive tax, levied only on the richest two per cent of society and contributing significant revenues to the public purse since 1916, was felled by a broad and powerful coalition that was successfully motivated by an essentially moral case for its abolition. Its demise is a lesson in the dangers of relying on statistical evidence and arguments from self interest in the face of powerful stories deployed in the service of moral reasoning. The Democrats argued that the tax would only be paid by the richest and that it was not in the majority interest to reform and repeal it. The Republicans argued that the tax was wrong in principle and must be abolished. The Republicans won hands down.[55]

At the moment the moral arguments against child poverty and the transmission of disadvantage are not effectively deployed. In part this is because a lack of empathy prevents them from resonating with a broad enough percentage of the population. We should not assume that they are ineffective, rather that they are dormant. In the recent German federal election perhaps the most effective aspect of the SDP campaign was the decision to attack flat taxes as wrong in principle – that the nurse would pay the same as the millionaire and that this would simply be wrong. We too must avoid the trap of making the case for progressive policies exclusively on the basis of enlightened self-interest. If we do so we risk abandoning the moral high ground entirely, and it is advantageous territory on which to stand.

Notes

1   This figure is based on a relative poverty measure, 60 per cent of median equivalised contemporary household income Before Housing Costs (BHC) (figures for 2003/04). Based on After Housing Costs, there were 3.5 million children living in poverty in 2003/04. Whilst the Commission is also concerned about income measured *after* housing costs, the government's targets for 2010 onwards are expressed in BHC terms only. See table 5 for further details of the measure used here.

2   Whether or not the government has met its target for reducing relative low income by a quarter between 1999 and 2005 will be known when the Department for Work and Pensions publishes *Households Below Average Income 2004/05* in the spring of 2006.

3   Cabinet Office 2003.

4   Modood 2005.

5   These issues raise wider questions about integration and inclusion in British society which we do not directly address here, but which are likely to become increasingly salient over the next few decades, as the ethnic composition of the population changes, with an increasing proportion of minority ethnic people forecast in the future.

6   Two good starting points for such an audit are the annual Department for Work and Pensions publications *Households Below Average Income* (HBAI) and *Opportunity for All*. See also the bibliography to this report.

7   Fabian Commission on Life Chances and Child Poverty 2005.

8   The organisations who kindly participated in our focus group research were the Allenscroft Project, ATD Fourth World, Birmingham Women's Advice and Information Centre, Single Parent Action Network, the Welsh House Farm Project and Windows for Sudan. The methodology for this research is outlined in Appendix C.

9   The data discussed here are presented in more detail, with references, in Part Two of this report.

10 Announced in August 1997, the Social Exclusion Unit was launched in December 1997, with a brief to bring together policies across government departments to help the most disadvantaged.

11 The restructuring of national insurance contributions (NICs) benefited low-paid workers through the introduction of a primary threshold and the abolition of NIC from the first pound once the lower earnings limit was reached.

12 Myck 2000. It is important to recognise that this work models entitlement rather than actual receipt of resources, as there is incomplete take up of means tested benefits. In addition, the size of relative gains and losses is sensitive to assumptions about what the tax and benefits system would have looked like in the absence of the government's actual decisions over the period. The original papers contain further information on these issues.

13 Brewer 2003. Once again this work models entitlement rather than actual receipt of benefits. See note 12.

14 Brown 2002.

15 Adam 2005.

16 Make Poverty History is an umbrella organisation representing hundreds of member agencies in the UK, and is part of the Global Call for Action Against Poverty (GCAP).

17 The Commission for Africa was launched by Tony Blair in February 2004. The Prime Minister and the other members of the Commission formally began their work at the first meeting of the Commission on 4 May 2004.

18 See, for example, Lister 2004.

19 The first Children's Commissioner for England was appointed in March 2005, to give children and young people a voice in government and in public life, especially the most vulnerable children and young people in society.

20 Joint Committee on Human Rights 2003.

21 An independent Equalities Review was established in 2005, chaired by Trevor Phillips, to investigate the causes of persistent discrimination and inequality in British society. It is due to publish its interim report in spring 2006. Parallel to the Equalities Review, the Department for Trade and Industry (DTI) has begun work on a Discrimination Law Review (DLR) to assess how anti–discrimination legislation can be modernised to fit the needs of Britain in the 21st century.

22 In the case of income, one commonly used summary measure of inequality is the Gini coefficient, which provides an indication of inequality across the whole distribution, and takes a value between 0 (everyone has the same income) and 1 (one person has all the income, and no one else has any). It is also common to compare the share of income received by the 20 per cent of lowest income households with that of the 20 per cent of highest income households. Other commonly used measures give the ratio between the income of households at two points on the income distribution, for example at the 10 percentile (where ten per cent of households have lower incomes) and the 90th percentile (where 90 per cent of households have lower incomes). The higher the 90/10 ratio (or the 75/25 ratio, etc.) the greater is inequality on this measure.

23 Between 1996/7 and 2003/4 the post-tax Gini coefficient for the UK remained stable, at around its peak level for the last 20 years. See Jones 2005.

24 See e.g. Blanden *et al.* 2005.

25 The third is the maintenance of a stable and growing economy, with low levels of inflation and interest rates and high levels of employment.

26 HM Government 2004.

27 The usefulness of different kinds of targets and standards in tackling inequality is discussed in more detail in section 3.2.

28 Marmot 2004.

29 *Ibid*, pp. 126-7.

30 *Ibid*, p. 132.

31 The analysis in Part Two explores inequalities in life chances across this broad range of dimensions, though it should be noted that we are unable to explore all in the same depth, due to constraints of time and space and because more empirical evidence exists for some areas than others.

32 Dworkin 1977, cited in Cohen, 2002.

33 Marmot 2004.

34 Rawls 1971, p. 179

35 These concepts were discussed at greater length in the Commission's interim report, *Life Chances – What does the public really think about poverty?*

36 Taylor-Gooby (2005) Attitudes to Social Justice

37 See http://www.mori.com/polls/trends/issues.shtml

38 Park *et al.* 2005.

39 Park *et al.* 2002.

40 Hedges 2005, Sefton 2005.

41 Hedges 2005.

42 Park *et al.* 2005.

43 *Ibid.*

44 There have in fact been no major increases in support for adults without children who are not in paid work under the Labour government.

45 The proportion of British respondents to the Eurobarometer surveys attributing poverty to laziness or lack of will power was noticeably lower in the early nineties, for example, than in the previous decade, while the numbers attributing poverty to social injustice peaked in 1993, at a time of economic recession and high unemployment. Gallie & Paugam 2002.

46 The Eurobarometer surveys have asked questions about perceived causes of poverty since 1976, distinguishing between personal causes of poverty ("because they've been unlucky" and "because of laziness or lack of willpower") and social causes ("because there's a great deal of injustice in our society" and "it's inevitable in the modern world").

47 One notable exception here is the exploratory qualitative study by Alan Hedges (2005) on public attitudes towards and perceptions of redistribution.

48 Feinstein 2003.

49 Ridge 2002. These issues are discussed further in section 2.4.4.

50 Sefton 2005.

51 See Hedges 2005 for a fuller elucidation of these reservations.

52 Sefton 2005, p. 28.

53 *Ibid.*

54 Hills 2004.

55 Graetz & Shapiro 2005.

Part Two:
Unequal chances

Introduction

Children in the UK have very different chances in life according to their different social and economic circumstances. This part of our report investigates the extent of these differences, tries to unravel some of the causal relationships at work, and considers the impact of government policy. Sections 2.2 to 2.5 consider four successive stages in children's development: the start of life; infancy and the early years; the period of compulsory schooling; and transitions post-16 to further and higher education, training and employment. Section 2.6 then considers poverty and the inequalities in the wider society that affect life chances.

Throughout a child's development their life chances are affected both by their previous experiences and by current factors such as their family circumstances. To help structure our thinking about these processes we identify four main sets of influences affecting children across the whole of their life course: first, parental and family factors; second, neighbourhood effects and public services; third, features of the social environment such as socio-economic inequalities; and fourth, wider public policy interventions.

At each stage in the life course it is possible to identify a number of key developmental issues that have particularly important effects on life chances. For example, at the very start of life a child's health is critical for it to have a good chance of achieving cognitive and emotional development in its early years, which is in turn critical for good social behaviour and attainment later on at school. In each case these outcomes are affected both by what has gone before and by the wider influences on the child. We can thus build up a life chances framework, illustrated in Figure 1 (right), that brings these different sets of influences together and indicates likely causal relationships with arrows.

Many of the processes by which some children have better and others have worse life chances can be readily identified, at least in a general way. For example, it is easy to see how more affluent parents will be able to bring their resources to bear to the benefit of their children. They can afford to live in better quality accommodation in safer, more prosperous areas, with better public services, transport links and amenities. Lower income families will be obliged to live where they can afford to, which may mean lower standards of housing, safety, transport or education.

But if the general nature of the relationship between such family characteristics and children's outcomes is widely known, it is much more difficult to understand exactly how things work in detail. There is still much to discover about the relative effects of specific factors, such as parents' income or education, and about the precise way that specific problems act to curtail opportunities.[1] Developing such an understanding is critical if we are to choose the right policy interventions.

The aim of this part of our report is therefore to identify the factors which influence children's development and to understand as best we can the nature of the processes – biological, social, and psychological as well as economic – by which inequalities are generated, compounded and passed on over time, from generation to generation, and from childhood to adulthood. We seek to explain *why it is* that the life-courses of different children appear to be set to a high degree by the time they are born, and to understand *why* at every stage pre-existing advantages and disadvantages tend to accumulate still further.

Thus, in section 2.2 we focus on the period between conception and birth and examine the factors affecting foetal development during pregnancy. In section 2.3, we examine the factors affecting development after birth, both in the home environment and outside the home, focusing in particular upon pre-school care and education. From the age of five, the most important source of stimulus outside the home becomes the school environment, which is the focus of section 2.4, while section 2.5 addresses children's outcomes at the end of compulsory education.

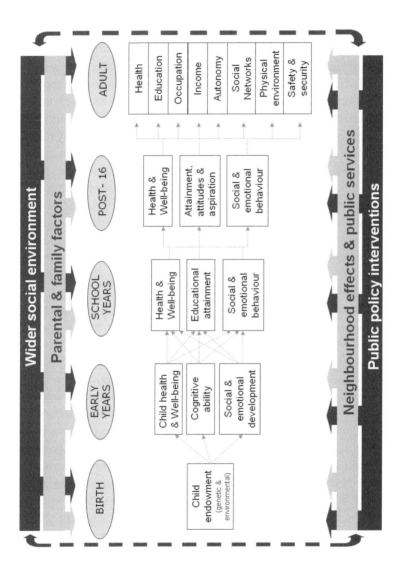

Figure 1
The life chances framework

For each phase of development we thus set out the key issues from a life chances perspective, examine parental and family influences on these, and then neighbourhood and policy effects. We then try to draw out the policy implications that will inform our recommendations in Part Three. We also draw upon the findings of some of the original qualitative research conducted for the Commission to illustrate the analysis. Where appropriate, we highlight what can be learned from people with direct experience of poverty about the way that poverty impacts upon children's development and also compare the experiences and outlooks of families on low incomes with those not living in poverty.

Finally, having charted the journey from infancy to childhood and into adulthood, in section 2.6 we turn to the question of how people's life chances are affected by wider inequalities, including inequalities of income, wealth and in the wider social environment, such as one's relative position in the social hierarchy.

A note of caution

It is important to sound a note of caution at this stage. There are a number of reasons why we do not have as clear an understanding of the causes of good and bad life chances, and of the effectiveness of specific policy interventions, as we would like. The first relates to the political context of the years from 1979 to 1997. On the one hand, at this time there was a lack of funding for research into childhood poverty and disadvantage, reflecting the low priority given to these issues by the governments of the day. On the other hand, social policy researchers found it necessary to devote their efforts to the more basic task of proving, in the face of ministerial reticence, the existence of problems such as social class gaps in health and education outcomes rather than researching the possible solutions.[2]

A second difficulty, and one which still applies in the currently more benign political climate, is the methodological problem of establishing causal relations rather than simply correlations in a very complex environment. Sophisticated techniques are needed to identify and separate the relative effects of different influences and to control for unobservable factors.[3] In many cases, the effects of related factors may be impossible to disentangle,[4] and the long-term effects of early childhood are difficult to establish, not least because of the difficulties of investigating sensitive areas such as the nature of family life and family relationships.[5] Part of the difficulty for researchers is that some outcomes are due to internal causes rather than external or environmental factors. For example, an outcome of interest such as child cognitive development may be correlated with two observable factors (such as parental income and parental education) which may both in turn be related to a third, internal factor, which is unobservable to the researcher.

As well as the complexity and sensitivity of the processes by which experiences in childhood affect outcomes in later life, an additional problem is the length of time it takes for effects to appear. In some cases, for example, we might specifically be interested in the effect of childhood interventions on adult outcomes such as employment rates. There is a necessary trade-off to be made therefore between charting these developments over time and being able to show the effects of contemporary policy decisions. In many cases this means that there is a lack of definitive evidence about the effectiveness of policy interventions, especially those that have been made since 1997. It is therefore usually necessary to act on the basis of the balance of probability, applying the available evidence within a reasonable theoretical framework. If we wait for certainty before taking action we may have to wait forever.

Inequalities at the start of life

2.2.1 Introduction

One of the most important shifts in public policy in the past eight years has been the increasing recognition of the importance of the early years of a child's life before they enter schooling. The primary reason for this has been the realisation that early intervention is particularly beneficial in terms of later child outcomes. However, whilst much attention has been given to childcare and pre-schooling, less has been given to the very start of life, including the period before birth, and the first year of life. Yet this time is critical for life chances, with children from different backgrounds facing significant inequalities at birth both in their prospects for surviving their first year in good health and for living long into retirement.

2.2.2 Infant mortality and low birth weight

Perhaps the clearest sign of inequality and disadvantage at birth is the class gap in low birth weight:[6] babies born to families on low incomes are significantly more likely to be born underweight (below 2500 grams) than the population as a whole.

- In England and Wales in 2002, the distribution of low birth weight babies varied by mother's age and father's socio-economic status (Figure 3), with parents in managerial and professional occupations having a lower chance of having a low birth weight baby than parents in routine and manual occupations in each age group.

- Analysis of the Millennium Cohort Study[7] reveals that parental unemployment, parental educational level and ethnicity are all significant contributors to low birth-weight.[8]

- Controlling for other factors, babies of Indian mothers are 3.42, Pakistani or Bangladeshi mothers 2.31 and Black mothers 1.79, times as likely to have a low birth weight as babies of White mothers.[9]

Low birth weight is significant from a life chances perspective because it is predicts chances of poor health and other problems in infancy and later life. First, low birth weight is linked to a higher risk of infant mortality: a baby born underweight is forty times more likely to die before her first birthday.[10] Second, being born underweight increases an infant's chances of experiencing developmental problems, such as low IQ, poor cognitive functioning and learning disabilities, and of exhibiting behavioural problems at school, even when parental social class and education are taken into account.[11] Thus, if we refer to the life chances framework in Figure 2, we can see that low birth weight is linked to poorer life chances in each of the three major domains of child development: child health, child cognitive ability and child emotional and social behaviour. Being born at a low birth weight casts a long shadow over children's prospects of flourishing for the rest of their lives.[12]

Despite medical advances and improvements in living standards, the first stage of life remains the most hazardous: mortality rates are highest around and just after birth and nearly 3,500 infants die before their first birthday each year in England and Wales. However, whilst overall infant mortality rates have improved, the rate of improvement has been slower for babies with fathers in manual occupations than the rest, causing the social class gap in infant mortality to widen.

- As Figure 4 shows, the infant mortality rate among children in lower social classes was double that for higher social class groups in 2000-02.

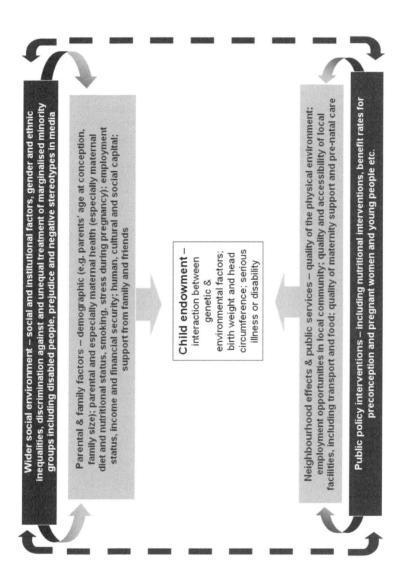

Figure 2
The Life Chances framework for the start of life

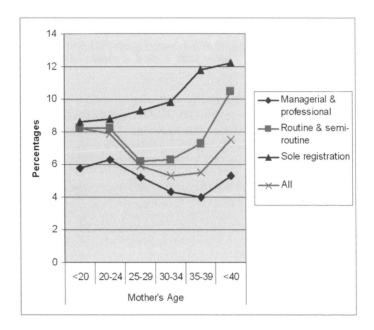

Figure 3
Percentage of low birth weight births, by mother's age, sole registration and father's socio-economic status 2002. *Source: Birth registrations, ONS.*

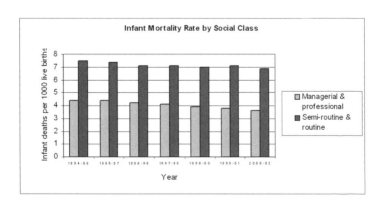

Figure 4
Infant mortality rate by social class. *Source: ONS 2004.*

- A social gradient in infant mortality exists across all classes: from four deaths per 1000 live births in social class I, to 5.4 in social class III (manual), 6.2 in social class IV and 8.1 in social class V.[13]

- The highest infant mortality rate during the period 1994 to 2002 was for babies registered by the mother alone (sole registration).

While some infant deaths can be attributed to congenital abnormalities and prematurity, the higher prevalence of low birth weight and infant mortality among working class groups is strongly linked to a number of risk factors associated with maternal health during pregnancy and prior to conception. Although there is much that we do not yet know or fully understand about the complex interaction of factors affecting foetal development,[14] one area of research where the evidence is strong is with regard to the connection between maternal health and low birth weight.[15] Maternal health and well being at the time of conception and through pregnancy is absolutely critical to the healthy development of the foetus. Starting with parental factors, we can say that two of the most important determinants of infant health are *poor maternal nutrition* and *smoking during pregnancy*.

2.2.3 Maternal nutrition prior to birth

The adequacy of a mother's diet during pregnancy is especially significant for children's life chances, as dietary deficiencies at this critical stage adversely affect foetal development and have long-term consequences for the healthy physical and mental development of the child. A meta-analysis of 277 English and French language studies published between 1970 and 1984 concluded that low birth weight was influenced by a number of nutritional factors, including pre-pregnancy maternal weight, gestational weight gain, energy intake, iron and anaemia.[16] Children whose mothers are underweight during pregnancy and at the time of conception have an increased risk of developing non-insulin diabetes and raised blood pressure in later life.[17]

59

Importantly for our purposes, research into low birth weight reveals a social class gradient in maternal nutritional status. Wynn *et al*'s (1994) study of a group of pregnant women in London found evidence of a social class gradient in the intake of protein, seven minerals and six B-vitamins, all of which were highly significantly correlated with birth weight. The findings also showed a strong association between babies who were born at low birth weight and with small head size and a nutritionally inadequate maternal diet at the end of the first trimester of pregnancy, which highlights the need to prioritise mothers' diet prior to conception, as well as during pregnancy. Similarly, a study of the diets of women on low incomes found that a third were deficient in their consumption of essential vitamins and minerals. Nearly half of the women ate no vegetables on a typical day, and three quarters consumed no fruit or fruit juice. The survey also found that many pregnant women on low incomes were missing meals, and importantly that those women with least money to spend on food were most likely to miss meals.[18]

As these studies indicate, parents-to-be living on very low incomes face obstacles to attaining a balanced, nutritious diet, not least of which is the cost of buying healthy ingredients. This is reflected in the perceptions of low income mothers themselves. As one mother remarked in our qualitative research with people with experience of poverty, *"when you're pregnant you need to have a healthy diet, but you can't afford a healthy diet if you're on benefits."* Another barrier to a nutritious diet for low-income households is lack of access to shops selling healthy food. These problems may be particularly acute for those living in areas which are not well-serviced by local shops ('food deserts'), and for the one in six households who do not own a car to drive to cheaper outlets sited away from residential areas. One pregnant mother who took part in our qualitative research indicated another problem related to income: she lacked the money to purchase basic cooking equipment, including an oven, on which to cook fresh, healthy meals at home and was therefore reliant on takeaways and microwave meals. The problem in this particular case was not any lack of knowledge of what constitutes a healthy

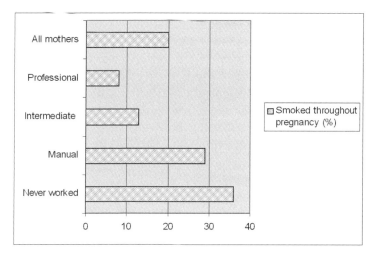

Figure 5
Percentage of mothers who smoked throughout pregnancy by mother's socio-economic status 2000. *Source: Infant Feeding 2000 for Department of Health, Scottish Executive, National Assembly for Wales and Department of Health, Social Services and Public Safety in Northern Ireland.*

diet so much as the material obstacles that prevented her from preparing and cooking nutritious food.

2.2.4 Smoking during pregnancy

A second major factor leading to low birth weight is smoking during pregnancy, which is known to have powerful effects on the life chances of the unborn child. Pregnant women who smoke are more likely to miscarry or to have pre-term deliveries than non-smokers, and are twice as likely to have low birth weight babies.[19] Their babies are more likely to die of sudden infant death, or to suffer from respiratory problems such as chest infections and asthma.[20]

According to the Health Development Agency (2003, p.1), smoking is the 'major modifiable risk factor contributing to low birth weight'. It is worrying, therefore, that the prevalence of smoking during pregnancy is greatest amongst mothers from lower socio-economic groups (see Figure 5).

- The Millennium Cohort Study confirms that children whose mothers smoke during pregnancy have a lower birth weight than children of non-smokers.[21]

- Black or Asian mothers are less likely to be smokers than white mothers.[22]

- While 20 per cent of all mothers smoke during pregnancy, 29 per cent of women in manual occupations and 36 per cent of women who had never worked were smokers in 2000, compared to 8 per cent of women in managerial and professional occupations.[23]

Things were not always so. Until the 1950s, smoking was something that was equally common in all social classes. Since then, public education campaigns promoting the message that smoking is dangerous to health appear to have been more effective in discouraging middle class people from smoking.[24] To understand why this class gap in smoking has opened up, we need to consider the reasons why people on lower incomes and in lower status jobs are more likely to indulge in health threatening behaviours, even when they are pregnant.

An important part of the explanation appears to lie in the pressures experienced by people on low incomes. Qualitative research conducted by Hilary Graham, which explored the health-related behaviour of a group of women on low income, found that for many women, smoking provided an outlet for the release of anxiety or tension. For these women, smoking was particularly difficult to give up, despite its known health risks, because it was viewed as their only relaxation, and as the only thing which they had for themselves, whereas the rest of their lives was devoted to looking after others.[25]

Further evidence as to why there is a social class gap in smoking is provided by analysis of the British Household Panel Survey (BHPS), which suggests that people who live and grow up in disadvantaged circumstances tend to have more fatalistic attitudes towards their health, and are more likely to view health outcomes as something that is impossible to control or change. It may thus be the case that disadvantaged young people are less likely to heed anti-smoking health warnings because they feel no control over their lives, and see little point in struggling to give up smoking for the sake of their health.[26]

None of this means that we should be any less assiduous in working to reduce smoking amongst disadvantaged groups, particularly young and pregnant women. However, understanding these kinds of pressures and attitudes will be important for finding the right smoking cessation interventions and for trying to reduce these pressures. In addition, our deliberative research indicated that at present when people are presented with evidence of class gaps in health-threatening behaviour they quickly assign blame. If we are to build public support for policies to close the gap in health outcomes it will be important to counter this tendency and to help the rest of the population understand what impact living in poverty really has on people.

2.2.5 Impact of the home environment

As well as differences in mothers' health-related behaviour during pregnancy, we also need to take into account the impact on maternal health and foetal development of the material circumstances and physical environment in which parents live during pregnancy – and prior to conception. Substandard accommodation and problems such as cold, damp housing lead to respiratory problems and other kinds of ill health, while unsanitary conditions may cause infectious diseases.[27] A sizeable social class gap also exists in exposure to environmental hazards that impact upon parental health and foetal development. Exposure to toxic agents such as radiation and poisonous metals such as lead, arsenic and mercury is much higher amongst lower income groups and has been shown to have deleterious effects on *in utero* brain development.[28] In addition, unsanitary conditions are linked to infectious diseases,

Substandard accommodation and a poor quality physical environment also create a different kind of health risk for pregnant mothers and their babies: as well as direct health effects (such as respiratory problems and infectious diseases), poverty and material deprivation may have indirect effects on foetal development by triggering biological stress responses in mothers which are passed on to babies before they are born. As recent research has revealed, maternal stress during pregnancy is linked both to reduced uterine blood flow (which leads to retarded growth in the uterus) and to higher cortisol levels for mother and baby. These biological stress responses are worrying, because high foetal cortisol levels are associated with higher rates of disease in later life.[29] In addition, there is clear evidence linking maternal stress to differences in the emotional behaviour of children in infancy and early childhood: a recent study of almost 7,500 children found that children whose mothers had been anxious or stressed during pregnancy had a much higher chance of developing emotional and behavioural problems by the time they were three years old than the children of non-stressed mothers.[30] Thus, along with maternal nutrition and smoking during pregnancy, a third major risk factor associated with low birth weight for infants is maternal stress during pregnancy, which affects babies' health and developmental outcomes even before birth.

What is important to emphasise here is the extent to which the health and well being of parents and parents-to-be are affected by external factors, including the stress caused by material deprivation and features of the home environment – and, as we shall see, the anxiety of having to get by and make ends meet on a very low income. The causes of maternal ill-health are not simply personal or individual factors, therefore, but wider societal factors; in particular, the chronic stress that is caused by poverty, social isolation, and feelings of inferiority and low status.[31]

2.2.6 Unequal access to maternity services

At the neighbourhood and community level, the most important factor affecting maternal health during pregnancy is access to high quality maternity services. Sizeable variation exists between ethnic groups in attendance at antenatal classes, which is correlated with a longer gestation period and a higher birth weight for babies. Attendance is lower for ethnic minority mothers than for white mothers, though attendance for all groups is still very low: 22 per cent of mothers of Asian children, 29 per cent of mothers of Black children and 33 per cent of mothers of children of mixed or other ethnic origins attend antenatal classes, compared with 40 per cent of mothers of White children.[32]

The Maternity Alliance finds evidence both of poor access to maternity care and poor standards of care for disadvantaged women.[33] Pregnant women on low incomes are likely to have greater difficulty in accessing antenatal facilities and services for a variety of reasons related to a lack of resources, such as the physical problems of accessing services in the absence of good public transport for those who cannot afford to travel by car, or because of difficulties in coordinating attendance with employment or with making childcare arrangements for existing children.

Problems of accessing proper maternity care are particularly acute for women from ethnic minorities, who are three times more likely to die in childbirth than white women. Maternity care for non-English speaking women is further hampered by communication difficulties with health professionals, which are exacerbated by problems in securing effective language support from independent interpreters. In short, high quality maternity services are not available equally to all women, and this lack of access and quality is a major cause of poor birth outcomes.[34]

2.2.7 Public policy considerations

Each of the risk factors identified above (maternal nutrition, smoking, environmental hazards, maternal stress, and unequal access to maternity services) is shaped by aspects of public policy. In the current UK policy context, there is a renewed emphasis on combating health inequalities and, as part of this, giving every child a healthy start in life is a high priority. The government has recognised that the health of mothers is the key to low birth weight rates, and that "two key interventions reduce the risk of low birth weight: promoting stopping smoking and optimum nutrition during pregnancy."[35] One of the two headline national targets on health inequality is to reduce the gap in infant mortality between manual groups and the population as a whole by 10 per cent by 2010.[36] The government is also committed to reducing the gap in adult smoking prevalence amongst lower routine and manual groups and the rest of the population to 26 per cent or less by 2010.[37]

The government deserves much credit for making the reduction of health inequalities central to its health policy. As we explore further, children's endowment at birth has consequences for their health and emotional and social behaviour as infants, which in turn has repercussions for their health and well-being in later life. However, although the government acknowledges that broader inequalities in life chances and living standards determine health inequalities, it has yet to embrace the challenge of tackling broader inequalities and the wider social determinants which are at the heart of health inequalities. In particular, it has so far paid less attention to two important sets of issues: first, ensuring that parents and parents-to-be have an adequate income to afford the cost of 'optimum nutrition'; and second, taking concerted action to address the wider social determinants of health, including the ill-health caused by chronic stress. At present financial support is targeted through the welfare benefits and tax credit system especially towards working adults and families with children. By contrast, workless adults, including many pregnant women and future parents, receive very low levels of adult benefit. It is also worth noting that Sure Start projects can now extend help and support to pregnant women as well as parents with children, though low-income pregnant women living outside Sure Start areas do not qualify for this kind of support.

Pregnant women on low incomes (who are receiving income support or tax credits)[38] are entitled to claim a Sure Start Maternity Grant, which provides a lump sum of £500 to help with the costs of the new baby. But not all eligible women are receiving the grant, as payment is conditional on claimants providing evidence that they have received health advice from a health professional (GP, midwife or health visitor).

Finally, while there is clear evidence of the linkages between maternal health and low birth weight, evidence of effective *interventions* to prevent low birth weight has been more difficult to establish. The Health Development Agency (HDA) recently reviewed the evidence on the effectiveness of a range of nutritional interventions, including vitamin and mineral supplements and nutritional advice.[39] Of the former, only calcium supplementation was shown to be effective, while evidence on the effectiveness of nutritional advice in pregnancy was conflicting – something that is not surprising, perhaps, given that knowledge of what constitutes a healthy diet is not the main problem. Similarly, evidence on the effectiveness of smoking cessation interventions to promote healthy foetal development is currently lacking, although the HDA review points the way towards efforts which focus on the smoking behaviour of partners and pre-conception interventions with mothers.

Accumulating disadvantage in early childhood

2.3.1 Introduction

One of the great political advances of the last few years has been the increased importance accorded to the early years of childhood. This has been reflected in policies such as Sure Start and commitments to more child-friendly employment law, as well as a broader political commitment on the part of Labour to improving support for parents and young children. The early years agenda appears to resonate with the public, and is developing into a central plank of Labour's wider political strategy.

At the same time, our understanding of the extent to which advantage and disadvantage accumulate during childhood has developed significantly due to numerous recent studies and policy evaluations. For example, it is now well known that in terms of their cognitive development, children who are born into less advantaged circumstances tend to fall behind in infancy and early childhood, while those who are born into relatively privileged positions tend to move ahead – in some cases overtaking children from less advantaged families who show early promise.[40]

The general policy conclusion and its key political implication are worth stating up front before investigating the detail. The central policy issue is that affluent parents with resources of social and cultural capital generally provide their children with a great start in their early years, whilst low- income parents and those with limited resources generally need significant support from public policy to do the same. The political point mirrors this: from a life chances perspective the early years agenda should principally be concerned with extending to disadvantaged children the opportunities which are already enjoyed by their more fortunate peers. Figure 6 sets out our framework for considering these issues in the period after birth, during infancy and before the start of schooling. Once again, we want to emphasise the interconnections between these different factors.

2.3.2 Parental and family factors

In this section, we draw out two of the most important factors which promote healthy development in the crucial first year after birth: breastfeeding and the formation of close attachments between parent(s) and child. We explain the importance of these for children's physical, intellectual and social development. We then try to account for the variation in breastfeeding rates amongst parents from different social classes; and examine the main factors in the home and wider social environment which affect parent-child relations.

The importance of breastfeeding for children's health and cognitive development

Breastfeeding provides an extraordinary range of health and developmental advantages for infants, so these variations are a real cause for concern. Breastfeeding for at least the first six months has been found to reduce the likelihood of infant mortality and to decrease the incidence and severity of many infections and allergies in infancy and later childhood. Compared with babies who are bottle fed, breast fed babies are at lower risk of childhood obesity and a wide range of diseases including cardiovascular problems in later life, and breastfeeding appears to act as a protective factor against the effects of low birth weight.[41] Breastfeeding is also associated with children's cognitive functioning and early neurological development, with breastfed children displaying significantly higher levels of cognitive function between six months and two years of age than those who are bottle fed.[42]

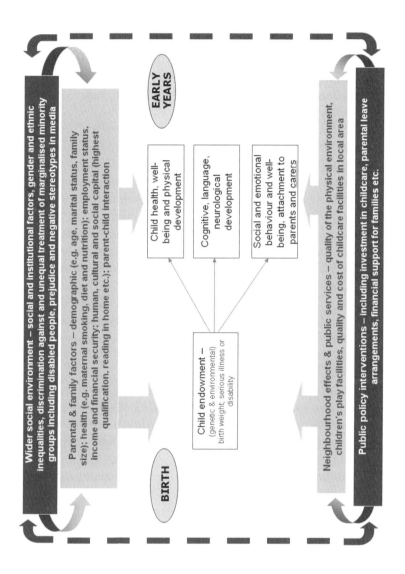

Figure 6
The life chances framework from infancy to the early years.

Socio-economic, regional and ethnic variations in rates of breastfeeding

- Mothers on low incomes are half as likely to initiate and maintain breastfeeding beyond six weeks as mothers on higher incomes.[43]

- The UK Infant Feeding 2000 Survey reveals a steep social class gradient in breastfeeding initiation in the UK, rising from 57 per cent of mothers in social class V to 91 per cent of mothers in social class I.[44]

- Regional variation also exists in rates of initiation in the UK, with initial breastfeeding rates at 71 per cent in England and Wales, 63 per cent in Scotland and 54 per cent in Northern Ireland.

- The Millennium Cohort Study reveals that, controlling for other factors, mothers from minority ethnic backgrounds are significantly *more* likely to initiate breastfeeding than white mothers.[45]

Why do these gaps in breastfeeding rates exist? Two important parts of the explanation are differences in maternal education and age. Mothers with higher educational levels (as well as those aged over 30 years) are more likely to initiate breastfeeding and to maintain it for longer.[46] This finding is consistent with a general pattern showing that maternal levels of education are positively correlated with health-related behaviours and children's health outcomes. One reason for this general pattern may be that mothers with low levels of educational attainment may lack basic skills, such as the capacity to follow written or oral medical and nutritional advice, while those with higher levels of attainment may be more proactive in seeking health-related advice and a better understanding of health-related behaviour. In addition, as discussed in the previous section, it is important to bear in mind the impact that living in poverty has on people's outlook and attitudes, engendering feelings of lack of control and fatalism about one's health.

Mothers' decisions about infant feeding are also likely to be influenced by their family and friends, and by the prevailing norms in the local community. Some working-class women grow up in a bottle-feeding 'culture', where breastfeeding is less likely to be practised, and where mothers, aunts and friends all tend to bottle-feed. In this kind of environment, there will be substantial family and peer pressure on new mothers to do the same, while advice and information from health professionals (e.g. home visitors, or in the hospital or Sure Start centre) is more likely to be resisted. Mothers who decide to bottle-feed rather than breastfeed report feeling worried about physical discomfort, and particularly about the social embarrassment they would feel having to breastfeed around others. One implication of these cultural factors for public policy is that it suggests the need for interventions, such as peer support projects, which aim to promote behavioural and cultural change in the local community, rather than focusing on individual mothers in isolation from their peer group.

The importance of parent-child interactions for children's intellectual and emotional development

From the earliest months of life, the pattern of interaction between parent and child has a lasting impact on multiple aspects of an infant's development. First, the quality of parent-child interactions matters for children's intellectual development. Neurologically, infancy is a critical period because cortical development is influenced by the amount of central nervous system activity stimulated by experience.[47] Linguistically, the development of children's vocabulary is affected by both the quantity and quality of parents' speech, and there is evidence of a sharp gradient of class inequality in parents' vocabulary and the way parents talk to their children within the home. One US study found that the average number of words infants heard per hour was 2,150 in professional families, 1,250 in working class families and 620 in non-working families.[48] Second, the quality of parent-child interactions has been shown to be an important protective factor against disadvantage: the relationship between parents and child has important effects for children's social and emotional behaviour, which in turn has knock-on effects for children's health and well-being.[49]

Recent research shows that there is a range of activities which have a positive effect on the development of children, as well as reducing their risk of special educational needs.[50] Certain activities, such as reading with the child, teaching songs and nursery rhymes, painting and drawing, playing with letters and numbers, visiting the library, teaching the alphabet and numbers, are important not only for increasing vocabulary and language skills, but also for distilling the idea that reading and education in general are important. In addition, taking children on visits and creating regular opportunities for them to play with their friends at home are all associated with higher social and behavioural scores.

Above all, what matters for children's intellectual, personal and social development is the extent to which parents are able to provide a stimulating and supportive environment for their children. Although parental education, income and occupation are all associated with children's development, (as parents with higher educational attainment and higher income may be better able to provide a stimulating environment), what ultimately matters more than these parental characteristics is the quality and nature of parent-child interactions.[51] As Sylva and colleagues (2004) express it, *'what parents do with their children is more important than who parents are'*.[52] This finding has obvious significance for public policy: it means that with the right support, low-income parents who themselves have low educational attainment can still 'improve their children's progress and give them a better start at school by engaging in activities at home that engage and stretch the child's mind'.[53]

The relationship between parental resources (educational, financial, social and cultural) and the quality and quantity of parent-child interaction is by no means straightforward. What matters is not just the amount of human capital (such as educational attainments) that parents happen to possess, but also the amount of *time* and *attention* they are able to give. This may be affected by family size, but also by difficulties such as physical illness or disability, mental illness, domestic tension and family breakdown (divorce or separation), as well as more serious problems such as alcoholism, and especially by the stress of living in poverty. The amount of time that parents spend with children will also depend on family decisions about childcare arrangements, which in turn will be affected by parents' income and occupation, and also by parental attitudes, priorities, and expectations.[54]

Finally, parents' ability to stay at home with their children will also depend on parental leave arrangements, including the provision of paid leave. Compelling evidence exists for the value of paid parental leave for mother and baby alike: paid parental leave is linked to a higher use of preventative health care and lower maternal depression, as well as to lower infant mortality and healthy childhood development. [55] Unpaid leave does not have the same protective effects, partly because of financial constraints prevent many from taking it up. There is a need to redesign the current policy approach to enable less well-off parents to spend more time with their children, and give them greater opportunities to nurture the capabilities and life chances of their children.

At present, women are entitled to six months of paid maternity leave and a further six months of unpaid leave, while men are entitled to two weeks of paid paternity leave. From April 2007 the paid period of maternity leave will be extended to nine months, as a first step towards the goal of twelve months paid maternity leave by the end of the current Parliament. As our qualitative research illustrates, the lack of paid maternity leave at present for the second six months of their year-long entitlement means that some new mothers feel as though they are forced back to work:[56]

> Women's group member: "I work full time, as well. And 'cos this is my first baby, I'll have six months maternity. And because I've been in my job a year, I get additional maternity, but that's unpaid. So basically how it's looking at the moment is, I'm having my first baby, but after six months I'll have to go back to work. I haven't got a choice really."

Recent improvements to maternity leave are therefore to be welcomed, as an important first step towards more generous allowances. But questions remain about the level of payment and the gender divide in parenting responsibilities within families. As well as being amongst the weakest in Europe,[57] equal rights campaigners have expressed concerns that statutory leave entitlements in the UK are more unequally divided between mothers and fathers than in any other European country.[58]

Under current proposals, paternity leave will be extended from two weeks through a maximum of 26 weeks, with statutory paternity pay at a flat rate of £106 a week for up to three months if the mother returns to work before taking her full entitlement. While any extension of paid leave is to be welcomed, it is not clear whether fathers will be sufficiently motivated to take up their new leave entitlements (which are in any case dependent on the mother's entitlement), given financial and other constraints, such as working practices and the culture in many organisations. It is therefore important to consider the level of payment, which needs to be high enough to allow all who want to take it to afford to do so.

The impact of poverty on child development

Low income impacts upon the life chances of parents and children in a variety of ways, one of which is via their physical and mental health. Poverty has adverse effects for families' diet and nutrition in a similar manner to pregnant women, and it also manifests itself in other forms of material deprivation. Parents on the lowest incomes have little choice about where to live and may have to live in substandard accommodation, in areas where the quality of the physical environment is very poor. The results of a national investigation into housing conditions in the UK by the housing charity 'Shelter' demonstrate that dirty, unsanitary and squalid housing conditions are linked to a wide range of physical ailments including asthma, respiratory tract infections, diarrhoea and vomiting, developmental problems, musco-skeletal problems, dental problems, skin conditions, a lowered immune state as a result of ongoing stress, and high rates of accidents. In addition, overcrowding and noise from neighbouring properties induce poor sleeping patterns. Living and growing up in substandard housing also increases the risk of suffering mental ill-health, including depression and chronic stress.[59]

Poor parental mental health is a key factor that may impair parent-child interactions and learning experiences in the home.[60] During the critical first months of life, babies born to low income and teenage mothers may be further disadvantaged by their mother's higher risk of suffering postnatal depression. Suffering from depression or other mental health problems can make it difficult for a mother to interact with her baby, affecting both the baby's emotional well-being and in the longer term the development of linguistic skills and reading ability. Worryingly, younger and lower-income mothers are less likely to be identified as suffering from post-natal depression despite the higher prevalence of the condition amongst these groups, and thus they have worse chances of accessing the support they need.

There is a growing body of evidence detailing how parents' capacities for parenting are adversely affected by the experience of poverty and the everyday reality of having to cope with life on very low income.[61] Poverty not only means a lack of financial resources, it also undermines individuals' capacities for parenting by depleting their personal reserves of energy and impacting on mental health and well-being, which affect their ability to cope with stressful or demanding events and circumstances. The pressure of having to 'get by' – that is, of having to make ends meet, day after day, on a very low income – may mean that when further difficulties arise (events that in normal circumstance would be stressful and worrying, but not excessively so) a person faced with financial uncertainty and insecurity may be unable to cope with the additional burdens these entail. In the words of one of our qualitative research participants, poverty is in this sense '*disabling*', because by exposing people to relentless pressure, it may undermine their capacity to deal with difficult and stressful situations.

The processes by which these effects are passed on from parents to children, and from early childhood to outcomes in later life, are both psychological and biological. First, given that early experiences are important in the development of personality traits, children may suffer the long-term psychological effects of trauma or stress in early childhood. Second, early experiences such as those associated with poor attachment between the baby and its parents, or the stress and anxiety caused by domestic conflict and poor family relationships, are known to trigger the same biological stress responses in children as are observed in babies before birth, leading to raised cortisol levels, which again have lifelong effects for health. In section 3.1 we saw how maternal stress in pregnancy has adverse effects on foetal development, and is linked to poor health and behavioural outcomes in childhood and in later life. As the work of Michael Marmot and Richard Wilkinson has done much to highlight, these negative effects continue after birth. Stressful early environments may also lead to higher blood pressure in childhood, which is predictive of higher blood pressure in adulthood.[62]

2.3.3 Childcare and pre-school education

Differences in the home environment and in parents' resources can thus be seen to have a major impact on children's life chances. However, differences in children's experiences *outside* the home also profoundly affect child health, cognitive functioning and emotional behaviour. The negative side of this story is that at present inequalities in the home environment are generally *compounded* by inequalities in the quantity and quality of care and education that children receive outside the home in early childhood. However, the positive side is that there is great potential for public policy to have an effect outside the home in a way that can redress some of the problems experienced within the home.

Besides being looked after by parents, young children may be cared for informally by close relatives or family friends, or more formally by child minders or nannies, or in centre-based nurseries and play groups.[63] Not all these options will be available in all places, and the actual range will depend on provision in the local area. Around 60 per cent of working mothers use some form of childcare, though this proportion is higher for mothers with younger children, and only a minority of working mothers use formal childcare.[64] Most parents prefer to use informal childcare such as is provided by friends and relatives, although formal childcare is used more for younger children.[65]

Importantly, disparities continue to exist in enrolment and participation amongst different social groups. Children with parents in professional or managerial occupations are more likely to attend nursery education, and to participate at an earlier age, than children from other social class backgrounds.[66] In particular, disadvantaged children tend to attend pre-school for shorter periods of time overall than those from more advantaged groups (around four to six months less).[67]

The impact of childcare on children's development: why inequalities in provision and uptake matter

There is a substantial body of evidence from US studies detailing the benefits of high quality, developmentally appropriate child care for toddlers and the pre-school years. Benefits are reported for children's social, emotional and, in some cases, linguistic development;[68] their verbal ability and reasoning skills;[69] and also for maternal outcomes including mental health, coping skills, knowledge about childrearing, and mother-child interactions.[70] There is also a growing evidence base in the UK, which confirms many of the US findings. In recent years, the Effective Provision of Pre-school Education (EPPE) project, a large-scale study of children in the UK, has investigated the effects of different types of pre-school education for children's intellectual and behavioural development.

The key findings are that pre-school experience enhances all-round development in children (improving cognitive attainment, sociability and concentration at the start of school), that these effects continue into primary school, and that they are still in evidence at the end of Key Stage 1 (i.e. age seven).[71] The study also provides evidence, however, that an early start in group settings, particularly before the age of two, led to slightly increased behavioural problems for a minority of children at age three and again at age five. The accuracy of this finding is contested, however, because parents' judgements about the behaviour of their children were retrospective. Above all, what matters for children's development and well-being is the *quality* of the experience.[72] Of particular importance is the relationship between child and caregiver, and especially the sensitivity and responsiveness of the caregiver, which is something that may be increased by training.

The EPPE findings also demonstrate that disadvantaged children benefit significantly from good quality pre-school experiences, especially where they interact with a mixture of children from different social backgrounds. In addition, pre-school education appears to have an important role in helping improve the outcomes of those with Special Educational Needs. As the authors conclude, whilst it does not eliminate differences in social backgrounds, pre-school 'can help to reduce the disadvantage children experience from some social groups and can help to reduce social exclusion'.[73]

In light of these potential benefits from high quality pre-school care and education, it is a matter of concern that childcare tends to be weakest where it is most needed and where improvements in children's outcomes could be greatest. As Meyers *et al* articulate it, children from less well-resourced backgrounds are 'doubly disadvantaged': that is, 'less likely to receive stimulation and needed resources at home, and less likely to attend the type of care that we know promotes school readiness'.[74] We would say that in many cases the disadvantage faced by children from low-income families may by tripled, as those who do attend centre-based childcare outside the home are likely to receive less expensive, lower quality care (due in large part to a low-paid and under-qualified staff) than their more affluent contemporaries.

What factors explain the class gap in enrolment?

Parents' use of childcare of different kinds will obviously depend on what is actually available in the local area, as well as on family and parental factors such as income. Despite the recent expansion of places, parents continue to face considerable problems in terms of lack of availability. Survey evidence of parental perceptions of the availability and quality of childcare in their local area reveals some improvements. In 1997, 56 per cent of parents of three year olds, and 54 per cent of parents of four year olds thought there were not enough nursery places available in their local area. By 2002 these proportions had improved some-what to 52 per cent and 49 per cent respectively, whilst still remaining high.[75] With regard to quality, whereas half of all parents thought the quality of childcare provision in their area was only 'fairly good' or worse in 1997, this proportion had decreased to 37 per cent by 2002. Despite these modest improvements, the lack of places remains a significant challenge – and a sizeable obstacle to maternal employment.

For many parents on low and middle income, even for families in receipt of the childcare element of the Working Tax Credit,[76] the most significant barriers to enrolling children remains the cost of childcare. Furthermore, for many parents, and for lone mothers in particular, other obstacles and difficulties will compound lack of provision and affordability. Some of these problems can be illustrated by the findings of our qualitative research with parents with experience of poverty. As one non-working lone mother expressed it, the problem of accessing childcare [in this case, childminders] was "not just the cost", but also numerous other difficulties arising from the practical arrangements for transporting and collecting children at the appropriate time:

> Woman 1: "For me, it's not just the cost, it's that there's one woman [childminder] who covers all of this area. There's one, and she'll drop to [a particular] school, but my kids don't go to that school, which means I'll have to go further out to find child minders for my children. And I'd need to find one at a time when I can drop the kids off before school."

These practical obstacles were particularly acute for larger families, with children of different ages:

> Woman 1: "If you've got kids of different ages, then it's just too difficult to find childminders. And a lot of them, you can't find a place with one childminder, so I'd have to find three, and I'd have to get to all of them."

> Woman 2: "Sometimes it's difficult to get one child to one childminder, so it'd be impossible to do three."

The lack of childminders was echoed by other parents from the same area. Indeed, another mother even remarked that *'Parents change schools where there are child minders'*. In addition, this participant expressed the view that it was not *worth her while* to go back to work full-time, because of the cost of paying for childcare, and because of the difficulty of combining paid work with fulfilling her role as a mother:

> Woman 3: "It's going to be too much, having to work nine to five, then coming home and making their dinner and because of the cost of everything, it's not worth my while."

Finally, another mother drew attention to the 'silly little things' that would really help her to combine paid work with childcare:

> Woman 4: "But, I've got to learn to drive to do that [access childcare], and people who are on income support have to learn to drive but can't afford to do it. So they've got no options but to stay in the house all day. So it would be nice if the government would pay for half the driving lessons (laughter). Silly little things like that would really help."

2.3.4 Public policy considerations

The government is committed to facilitating increased parental use of formal childcare (e.g. in nurseries or play groups), both to promote maternal employment and because of its benefits for children's development. This area of policy has seen very significant developments under New Labour, from the launch of the first National Childcare Strategy in 1998 and the introduction of Sure Start, to the publication of the Ten Year Childcare Strategy in December 2004 and the introduction of Children's Centres.[77]

1.2 million childcare places have been created since 1997 (an increase in the net number of places of 525,000) in a range of settings including nurseries, with child minders and in before- and after-school clubs. Day nursery places have doubled since 1997 and after-school places have tripled.[78] However, it has proved more difficult to sustain childcare places once they have started-up, in part because of problems in the childcare market which are outlined below.

There is clear evidence that the quality of childcare matters most for improving child outcomes – and that what matters most for determining quality is a well-qualified workforce. The government has now acknowledged the need to raise the qualifications of the childcare workforce, and has committed resources to provide a £125 million a year Transformation Fund to support quality improvements in 2006 and 2007. Whilst these resources are welcome, they need to be set alongside the recognition that the workforce is both large and on average currently poorly qualified, so there is a problem of both the flow of workers into childcare and a bigger problem of the stock of the existing workforce. As in the case of the NHS, many years of higher spending will be required to address many previous years of inadequate resources.

The government has chosen to rely heavily on the Childcare Element of the Working Tax Credit (WTC) as the method of funding childcare for low income families. In theory, the advantage of this is that it puts the power in the hands of the parents, who can then choose the provider that best suits them. Making parents the purchasers of childcare is thus meant to stimulate supply and drive up quality. However, the childcare market is subject to a number of problems. The supply of skilled workers is relatively constrained, the costs of setting up a childcare enterprise are relatively high, demand is unpredictable, and as a result there is a lot of 'churning' of providers going in and out of business. It is also difficult for parents to acquire good information about the quality of childcare, and overall satisfaction with the quality of care does not seem to have improved very much in recent years despite significantly increased public resources.[79] There are also problems with the childcare element of the WTC itself, as the annual system of financial assessment creates inflexibilities, and because there is a maximum percentage and a maximum limit to what parents receive, leaving some parents, especially in London, unable to afford to meet the remaining costs themselves.[80]

In addition, the most disadvantaged parents, for example those with poor basic skills, are likely to find the process of accessing and paying for care in this way the most challenging.

For all of these reasons it will be necessary for the government to continue to play a significant role in the childcare market, ensuring both the supply of skilled workers, regulating standards, stimulating demand and where necessary directly providing services.

At present it is difficult to evaluate the success of the government's Sure Start programme of support for young children in disadvantaged areas. Too much has been made of early impact evaluations which failed to demonstrate significant benefits other than warmer parent/child relationships,[81] and media reports of apparently similarly inconclusive results from more recent evaluations.[82] We should be cautious about drawing premature conclusions about the impact of Sure Start, because of problems with the research design, which has examined child outcomes in Sure Start areas, rather than outcomes for children who have actually attended Sure Start programmes. We should also be cautious because of the inherent difficulties of trying to demonstrate so early the effectiveness of a project which is supposed to have impacts over the long term on child and then adult outcomes, and because local variations in parental input and innovation makes it difficult to draw conclusions at a national level. Both the theory and the relevant evidence suggest that high quality childcare and early years support pay long-term dividends and can help close the class gap in life chances.[83] Furthermore, existing research shows that parents report high levels of satisfaction with Sure Start. We should therefore hold our nerve and continue to support the development of the services in the UK as a permanent part of the welfare state. Improving the extent to which children from disadvantaged backgrounds experience high quality childcare in their early years is one of the central challenges for public policy from a life chances perspective. Another is to address the wider social determinants of poor child outcomes, an issue to which we will return in section 2.6.

Widening inequality of outcomes for school-age children[84]

2.4.1 Introduction

By the time children start school, stark inequalities between children from different social backgrounds are already evident in standard tests of development. The class gap in educational outcomes continues to widen throughout the years of compulsory schooling, with long-term consequences for later life chances. As qualifications are so important for subsequent life chances, the natural focus of the life chances agenda for school age pupils is the attainment of measured skills and formal qualifications in a school setting. Young people who leave school with low qualifications have a higher risk of unemployment, worse health outcomes, and a higher risk of poverty in later life.

Nevertheless, it is worth sounding a note of caution about focusing exclusively on qualifications and measured skills.[85] Children develop important assets and capacities that are not very effectively measured in tests, such as social skills, friendship networks and cultural capital. Young people with similar qualifications may thus have very different prospects, and indeed 'soft skills' appear to be a significant explanation of why young people from higher socio-economic status backgrounds often do better than their similarly qualified peers from less advantageous origins.[86] It is important not to lose sight of these issues whilst trying to drive up standards in terms of formal qualifications.

The focus on qualifications and attainment in school Key Stages also partly reflects methodological limitations: we focus on measurable skills and formal qualifications precisely because we lack data about educational outcomes which are more difficult to measure. Finally, it must be remembered that the school years are not simply important because of their later effects, but also form a period in the lives of young people which is valuable in and of itself. It follows that it is important to address the way in which inequalities can translate into differential experiences of school, and to ensure that education is an inclusive experience for *all* pupils including children in poverty.[87]

Our framework for life chances during the school years thus tries to remind us to avoid being too instrumental.

2.4.2 Educational outcomes and inequalities

Average school standards have risen significantly on a number of measures over the past decade. For example, there has been a general increase in the proportion of pupils achieving the benchmark of five GCSEs at Grade A* to C in England (from 41 per cent in 1992/93 to 53 per cent in 2002/03). Nevertheless, a strong relationship persists between parental socio-economic status and child attainment. The GCSE data in Figure 8 is just one example of this pattern, and similar outcomes are observed at earlier stages of the school career.

England & Wales				Percentages	
Social class	1992	1998	NS-SEC	2000	2002
Managerial/Professional	60	69	Higher professional	74	77
Other non-manual	51	60	Lower professional	61	64
Skilled manual	29	40	Intermediate	45	52
Semi-skilled manual	23	32	Lower supervisory	35	35
Unskilled manual	16	20	Routine manual	26	32
Other	18	24	Other	24	32

Note: Social class from 1992 to 1998, and NS-SEC from 2000 to 2002.

Table 1
Attainment of five or more GCSE grades A* to C: by social class/NS-SEC1, 1992 to 2002. *Source: Youth Cohort Study, Department for Education and Skills.*

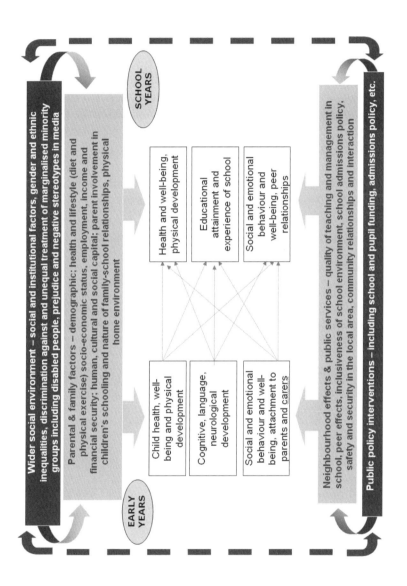

Figure 7
The life chances framework for the school years.

- In 2002, more than twice the proportion of children with parents in professional/managerial occupations in England and Wales gained five or more higher grade GCSEs (77 per cent) than children with parents in routine manual occupations (32 per cent) (See Table 1).

- This represents a welcome improvement since the previous decade: in 1992, children of parents in managerial and professional occupations were almost four times more likely to get five or more GCSEs at grades A*-C (60 per cent) than children of parents in unskilled manual jobs (16 per cent) (Table 1).

- However, while the ratio has improved significantly from the early 1990s, the scale of educational inequality represents a tremendous injustice to children denied equal life chances on the basis of their family background (Figure 8).

- Although average educational attainment at GCSE level improved for all ethnic minority groups between 1992 and 2002, performance data shows that particular groups achieved disproportionately better outcomes than others (Figure 9).

- Chinese and Indian children outperformed all ethnic groups (Chinese children are represented in Figure 9 in the 'Other Asian' category).

- Bangladeshi children have shown the largest improvement over the last decade with an increase of 27 percentage points from 14 per cent in 1992 to 41 per cent in 2002.

- Among girls, pupils of Pakistani origin start off as one of the poorer progressing groups at Key Stage 2 (age seven to 11), but at GCSE they are one of the best progressing groups.[88]

- In contrast, Black pupils showed the least improvement with an increase of 13 percentage points. Regardless of gender or FSM status, pupils of Black Caribbean origin make below

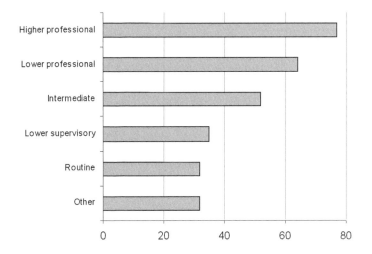

Figure 8
Attainment of five or more GCSE grades A* to C: by parental NS-SEC, 2002.

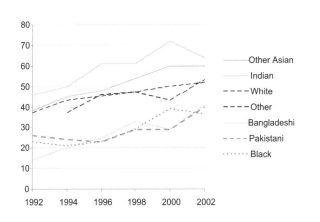

Figure 9
Attainment of five or more GCSEs grades A*-C: by ethnic group, 1992-2002.

average progress at all Key Stages, despite entering the school system generally with above-average educational attainment.[89] Some of the reasons for these trends are discussed further in section 2.6.8.

The standard way to examine socio-economic inequalities in educational attainment is to use entitlement to free school meals as (FSM) an indicator of social disadvantage.[90] Comparisons of the results of FSM pupils with non-FSM pupils have certain limitations. First, being eligible for FSM is really an indicator of family poverty rather than a measure of social class: given that not all working class households qualify for state benefits, the proportion of FSM pupils in a school is not an accurate indicator of its overall class composition. In addition, results will vary depending on whether entitlement to FSM or receipt of FSM is being measured. One problem with using *take-up* off FSM rather than eligibility is that evidence exists of 'cultural differences in the willingness of some communities to take advantage of state benefits', which may produce anomalies in research.[91] Nevertheless, in the absence of systematic data about the income and social class of pupils, information about FSM status provides a useful (though flawed) proxy of social disadvantage.

In general terms, schools with a high proportion of pupils entitled to free school meals (indicating a more deprived intake) do less well overall than schools with a low proportion (indicating a more affluent intake). However, this broad finding masks a much more complex picture of educational inequalities at the individual pupil level. Recent research by the Department for Education and Skills helps us explore the changing pattern of results in primary schools at the end of Key Stage 2, by comparing test scores for the years 1998 and 2004.

- Since 1998, primary schools with the highest proportion of FSM pupils have seen the biggest increases in the proportion of pupils achieving the expected standard of Level 4 + at Key Stage 2 (see Figure 10).

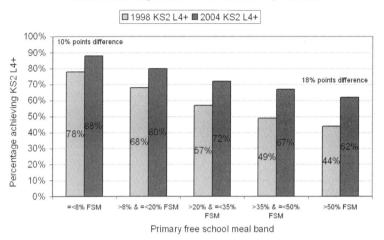

Figure 10

Improvements in KS2 Level 4+ English results for schools with different proportions of pupils eligible for free school meals.

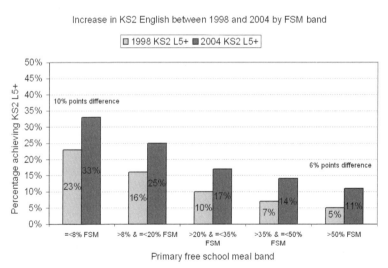

Figure 11

Improvements in KS2 English results using the Level 5+ performance measure.

- However, the situation is reversed for the more demanding performance standard of Level 5+, where schools with the least deprived intakes have made more progress (see Figure 11).

- Thus, whilst progress is being made in deprived schools, more affluent schools are nonetheless pulling ahead at higher levels of performance.

Key Stage 2 English (APS analysis)	Pupil classsification	
	Non-FSM	FSM
1998 mean average point score	26.2	23.5
2004 mean average point score	27.5	24.5
Change in points 1998 – 2004	+1.3	+1.0

Key Stage 2 Maths (APS analysis)	Pupil classsification	
	Non-FSM	FSM
1998 mean average point score	25.7	22.9
2004 mean average point score	27.6	24.6
Change in points 1998 – 2004	+1.9	+1.7

Table 2
Improvements in pupil mean average point score, for FSM and non-FSM pupils. *Source: DfES.*

At the individual pupil level the picture is also worrying. Average point scores for pupils at Key Stage 2 have gone up both for pupils who are entitled to free school meals and those who are not. And yet, despite the initially higher scores for pupils not entitled to free school meals (and therefore less 'room for improvement'), the gap between the two groups has slightly widened between 1998 and 2004.

- Whilst schools with more deprived pupils have generally seen their average results improve faster than schools with less deprived pupils, the pupils who are entitled to free

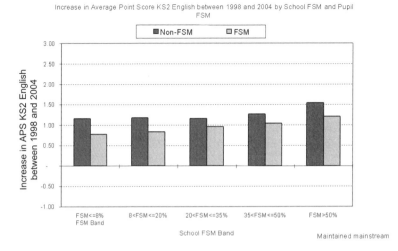

Figure 12

Improvements in average point score for pupils in schools with different levels of FSM: English. *Source: DfES.*

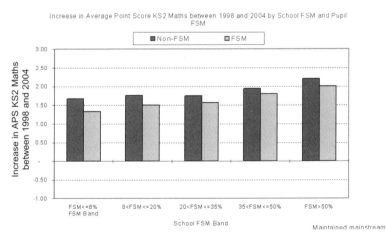

Figure 13

Improvements in average point score for pupils in schools with different levels of FSM: Mathematics. *Source: Df\ES.*

school meals have improved more slowly than their peers within each band of deprivation.

- As Figures 12 and 13 illustrate, improvements in schools with disadvantaged intakes are thus concentrated among the less deprived pupils.

2.4.3 Parental and family variables

There are numerous ways in which parents on higher incomes can use their economic and financial resources to benefit their children's education. This occurs directly, for example by investing in the smaller class sizes, better equipment and other advantages offered by private schools, and indirectly, for example, by moving house to live in the catchment area of a high-performing (and therefore frequently oversubscribed) school in the state sector. Parents with higher disposable income are also better placed to supplement their children's schooling with additional education, for example by paying for tutoring or extra music or drama lessons.

Parents' resources also affect their ability to be involved in their children's schooling.[92] Attendance at parent-teacher meetings, for instance, requires parents to make arrangements for transportation and child care, as well as requiring flexibility at work – resources which are more likely to be available to parents on higher incomes and with greater autonomy in the workplace. The pressure to be involved in children's schooling creates particular strains for lone parents, especially at a time when there are growing expectations that they should be in paid work.

Parents who themselves have low educational attainment may have difficulties in assisting their children with homework. Particular problems are experienced by immigrants whose first language is not English, as they may face both linguistic and cultural barriers to supporting their children's schooling.

During our qualitative research, in a discussion with a group of refugees and asylum seekers, parents expressed anxiety and frustration about not being able to support their children with their school work, either because of their own limited command of

English, or because they did not fully understand the education system in this country:

> "...some don't know much English, but some parents even if they know English, they don't know the system, so it becomes very difficult, because parents try and teach the children the way they were taught at home, and the children reject it, and say, 'No, it isn't taught that way in school'."

Class differences also exist in resources such as networks of friends and social acquaintances.[93] Research suggests that middle-class parents are more likely to be in contact with other parents and to share information about the school, for example about the reputation of individual teachers and the academic progress of their children.[94] In addition, the higher levels of status and prestige associated with higher salaried and professional occupations may help build confidence to monitor and criticise teachers. By contrast, some parents from disadvantaged backgrounds find it very difficult to approach teachers, because their own negative educational experiences have alienated them from the world of education.[95] Social class and family background therefore influences the social, educational, monetary and informational resources that parents bring to the family-school relationship.

Finally, some parents may be better placed to make use of their personal resources and social contacts to improve the educational prospects of their children. This may be especially important for low-achieving children from higher income families, as their parents are reputedly more likely to press the school authorities to test their child for recognised learning disabilities and special educational needs. Thus, they are more likely to seek a diagnosis of a condition such as dyslexia or attention deficit disorder that requires specialist treatment, rather than simply accepting or assuming that their children are just less able.

Drawing on her personal experience of living in poverty and from many years of experience working with women and families in poverty, one women's group leader talked about the difference she perceived in the resources and opportunities available to parents from different social classes:

"What I've come across is massive inequalities, so that if you're from a middle class family and you live in a decent area with your school, you will know that your child has an IQ of 136 and he has learning disabilities, because you have the resources and the opportunity to find that out. But if you live in a crap area, you've just got a thick kid basically. You don't have the human resources, because you're that drained by other things in your life anyway, so survival is your priority, not whether your kid ever gets a GCSE. So it's rare to come across somebody who does know."

The issue of parental involvement also raises an important question about the extent to which parents can offset the harmful effects of living in poverty. This question is addressed by Darcy Hango (2005), using data from the National Child Development Study (NCDS) to explore the relationship between parental involvement, poverty in childhood and later educational attainment. His analysis suggests that parental involvement acts as a 'partial' mediator, helping to compensate for some of the detrimental effects of lack of resources, but without cancelling the negative association between poverty and education completely.[96]

The physical and material circumstances in which children grow up affect their health, physical development and well-being in different ways, and may impact upon their levels of concentration in the classroom or their ability to study at home. Children growing up in households on very low incomes are less likely than their peers to receive a healthy, balanced diet, because of problems in accessing and affording healthy food. As Jamie Oliver's 'Feed Me Better' campaign to improve the quality of school dinners has recently highlighted, food of poor nutritional quality affects pupil behaviour and their ability to concentrate in the classroom and so has deleterious effects for their educational performance.[97]

Furthermore, families with the lowest incomes have very limited choice about where to live and may be forced to live in substandard accommodation. Poor quality housing impacts upon children's life chances in multiple ways. First, it is linked to a higher prevalence of diseases such as respiratory problems. Indeed, the British Medical Association states that multiple housing deprivation poses as 'serious a risk to health as smoking, and has been shown to be more harmful than excessive alcohol consumption'.[98] Besides the direct impact on families' physical health, poor quality housing also has a significant impact on families' well-being, affecting the mental health and emotional well being of parents and children alike.[99] The housing charity Shelter highlights the deleterious effects of overcrowding on children's ability to study at home, and on their social networks and friendship. Particular difficulties are faced by those 'homeless' families who are placed in temporary accommodation, due to a shortage in permanent housing – something which now affects over 100,000 households, including 116,581 children in England.[100] Evidence from Shelter's national investigation into housing for families suggests that having to make frequent moves between temporary accommodation has adverse effects for children's school work and intellectual development. One estimate is that homeless children miss on average a quarter of their schooling.[101]

A further pathway through which income affects children's life chances is through the adverse effects of financial insecurity within families. For older children in particular, family economic pressure is associated with conflict between children and parents, lower school attainment, reduced emotional health, and impaired social relationships. Importantly, some researchers suggest that rather than poverty or low income *per se*, the source of conflict between parents and teens may be income loss or economic uncertainly due to unemployment and unstable work conditions.[102]

The impact of financial insecurity on children and young people may help to explain the strong relationship between family income and mental disorders in childhood. The first large-scale national survey of child mental health in the UK, carried out by the Office for National Statistics in 1999, found that ten percent of children aged five to fifteen experienced handicapping emotional or behavioural problems.[103] Significantly, children living in families with a gross weekly income of under £100 were almost three times as likely (16 per cent) to have a mental disorder than children in families earning £500 per week or more (6 per cent). The study also found evidence of strong links between housing quality and children's mental health: in 1999, children living in social sector accommodation were nearly three times more likely (17 per cent) to suffer from mental illness than those in privately owned housing (6 per cent). Mental ill health and emotional or behavioural problems are particularly worrying from a life chances perspective, because they are related to various short- and long-term negative outcomes, notably disrupted schooling, stigma and discrimination, and social isolation.[104]

2.4.4 Children's experience of childhood

If, as we have seen, parental involvement can help to compensate for lack of economic resources, what role can schools play in breaking the link between family background and children's life chances? In theory, schools have a powerful role to play in helping children to overcome the effects of early disadvantage, by providing opportunities and experiences that they might not otherwise have. Too often in practice, however, social disadvantage appears to be compounded by educational underachievement. Indeed, instead of preventing the accumulation of advantage and disadvantage, some features of the current education system may even entrench inequalities.

At an institutional level, we need to acknowledge the role of private education in reinforcing privileged life chances. Although the political barriers to reform at present appear insurmountable, it is nevertheless important to recognise the extent to which the existence of an academically-selective, fee-paying private school sector magnifies the effects of parents' widely differing financial resources.[105]

Research in the social sciences in the past thirty years has contributed to our understanding of the social processes inside the school and the ways in which wider social inequalities are reproduced through the school's organisational model, the content of the curriculum, the style of teaching and relationship between teachers and students in the classroom.[106] For example, sociologists of education such as Basil Bernstein have used ethnographic research to study the nature of classroom learning, and have shown how the language used in textbooks and by teachers in the classroom may benefit children from middle class families at the expense of working class children. In this way, early advantages and disadvantages in the vocabulary that children acquire at home may be compounded by the patterns of language used in schools.

A further source of stress and anxiety for low-income families is that lack of income may be a barrier to children fitting in at school and participating fully in school life. Research shows that teachers may not always be aware of the embarrassment and humiliation that children feel when they are treated insensitively, for example in the way that free school meals are administered or if parents cannot afford to pay for extra-curricular school activities such as school trips.[107]

Children also come under pressure to keep up with their peer group in having fashionable clothes and other items, especially from advertising (such as that during Saturday morning television or at tea time) aimed directly at their age-group.[108] According to a recent report by the National Consumer Council, young people report that intrusive and inappropriate adversising makes them feel uncomfortable, pressurised and stressed. Health campaigners and consumer activists have also highlighted the marketing of food and drinks products to young consumers, linking the selective targeting of children by fast food chains to rising childhood obseity.[109] Although evidence of the direct effects of advertising on food consumption is disputed,[110] there is growing evidence of the adverse effects of growing consumerism on children's happiness and mental well-being.[111]

As mentioned in section 1.4.2, growing commercialism was identifed by participants in our deliberative research as one of the major changes in society affecting the experiences of children today. However, while a number of participants lameted what they saw as a trend towards increasing materalism, there was much less understanding amongst the group of the stress and stigma that lack of consumer goods can bring.[112] For those who have not experienced it, lack of income to afford the 'right' clothing may seem like a peripheral issue. But in reality it can mean a failure to fit in with one's peer group, and an increased risk of being bullied or otherwise excluded.[113] Although media coverage of bullying-related incidents in schools has raised the profile of the issue in recent years, the link between bullying and poverty has not been given the same emphasis, and demands wider publicity to promote greater public awareness.

2.4.5 Public policy considerations
The extent to which children's educational outcomes are shaped by features of the educational system in turn depends on political decisions about schooling. A key issue for public policy is whether the major determinant of school outcomes is the quality of intake, or whether higher spending on schools leads to better quality teaching (and therefore better results for pupils).

School admissions policy: improving the quality of intake
There is robust evidence of strong peer group effects in schools, with clear advantages accruing to pupils that attend schools with a more affluent intake.[114] Quality of intake is particularly important from a life chances perspective, moreover, as the effect is stronger for pupils from lower social class backgrounds. In the UK, however, schools are relatively socially segregated. Around a third of all children in England and Wales would have to change establishment for there to be an even distribution of low income children between schools.[115]

'Parental choice' has been a central tenet of the UK admissions system since the introduction of the Education Reform Act (ERA) in 1988. Its virtues were extolled under the Conservatives as part of a wider strategy to encourage local school autonomy and to undermine the role of the Local Education Authority (LEA). Under Labour, 'parental choice' has been linked to the aim of encouraging a greater social mix of students, so that school admission is not simply on the basis of a school's geographical catchment area. And yet, critics of the current admissions system deny that parental choice exists in any meaningful sense at all. It has certainly not significantly reduced the degree of social segregation in schools over the past eight years. This is partly because transport arrangements mean that the local school is the only feasible option for many parents. What happens in practice, moreover, is that popular and successful schools tend to be over-subscribed and so have greater discretion over admissions. This has led to claims that popular state schools now select on proximity rather than ability, as over-subscribed schools end up with such small catchment areas that only the rich can afford to live there.[116] The worry, therefore, is that the policy of parental choice is a façade because of the premium it places on parents' information and resources.

The current system of school admissions has impacted on the balance of intake within schools. There is evidence that low-income children have become increasingly concentrated in particular schools over the last five years, leading to schools in deprived areas having to cope with greater concentrations of disadvantaged pupils.[117] A recent study found that the intake of the highest performing schools tends to be unrepresentative of the local area, having fewer pupils entitled to FSM than the surrounding area.[118] Thus, as well as looking at parents' capacities for decision-making about school applications, it is also important to stress the constraints of the system in which parents make 'choices'. Although reforms since 1997 have led to greater diversity in types of school in the state sector, whether or not parents are able to send their children to a particular type of school depends strongly on where they can afford to live.

In short, the 'choice' of school available to children and their families is by no means equal. Instead, the options available to children depend very much on their families' particular circumstances. Part of the difficulty in tackling educational inequality is that the 'strategies' deployed by parents on behalf of their children simply reflect their deeply held wish, as parents, to improve the life chances of *their own children*. As the educationist Peter Mortimore observes, the issue is complex, because the desire of parents to promote their children's best interests, as they see them, is perfectly understandable. But a system that encourages parents 'to think *exclusively* of what is best for their children' has led to a 'rising tide of dissatisfaction and a lengthening list of those appealing about their failure to obtain the school of their choice.' Instead, we need 'to consider what is best for our society as a whole'.[119] This raises difficult political questions about how to communicate this message more widely –

and whether policies to promote parental choice may have the unfortunate effect of exacerbating the tendency to view 'life chances' individualistically, in a socially divisive rather than socially inclusive way.

Whilst we believe that achieving a more balanced pupil intake will be a key issue for addressing educational inequalities, it is also worth recognising some of the tensions between this objective and the idea of a school as one of the key centres of its geographical community. Residential areas are themselves relatively segregated by income, ethnicity and class, so in the short-term a balanced intake policy would require many children to attend schools outside their local area. A longer-term objective, however, must be to consider how housing policy can be revised to reduce social segregation and achieve a better mix of income, ethnic and class groups.

School funding: addressing the quality of teaching

With regard to the quality of *teaching*, one obvious way to address educational inequalities is to shift financial resources towards disadvantaged groups. This could operate on at least three levels, through the distribution of funds: from central government to Local Education Authorities; from LEAs to schools; and within schools, to more disadvantaged pupils. The 2004 Child Poverty Review signalled that the government would investigate the relationship between the level of disadvantage experienced by schools and the level of funding they receive through national and local funding formulae, but the results of this have not yet been published.[120] If we are to make serious inroads into educational inequalities, it is essential that the schools in the most disadvantaged areas are run by the best head teachers, and have the best staff working with the most disadvantaged pupils. This may mean developing more effective financial incentives for teachers and head teachers, and better measures of teacher performance.

One key use of additional resources in schools would be to reduce class sizes selectively. The 1997 Labour manifesto promised to reduce primary school class sizes to 30 or under for all five, six and seven year-olds. Whilst this may have been politically attractive, there is little evidence that it improved child outcomes. In fact, research suggests that small changes in class size have little effect on attainment, whilst large cuts do improve outcomes particularly for disadvantaged pupils.[121] If resources are to be focused on cutting class sizes, therefore, then the priority should be on large cuts in deprived areas rather than smaller cuts spread more widely. This would reflect the greater need of the deprived areas, but also that small reductions might have little effect in more affluent areas. A more radical approach would be to actually allow class sizes to rise in more affluent areas to fund cuts elsewhere.

Perhaps the most difficult issue is targeting resources on disadvantaged children within the school and within the classroom. The government now has an opportunity to frame its ambitions for 'individualised learning' around educational inequality. This could encompass special support and additional activities both for pupils who have fallen behind, and for those who can be considered at risk because of their home circumstances.

In addition, government arguably has a role to play in promoting an inclusive school experience, by helping parents to meet the 'hidden' costs of schooling. Research by the DfES in 2003 suggests that average annual spending by parents on pupils attending state schools is £948.11 for secondary school pupils and and £563.15 for primary school pupils. This spending includes the costs of paying for school dinners, school uniform and sports equipment, school trips and other events. A recent report on the cost of a 'free' education, co-authored by 11 children's charities, highlights the problems this can cause for low-income families.[122] Legally, schools can only ask for 'voluntary contributions' for school trips, and yet parents report being put under pressure to meet these costs, which causes stress, anxiety, guilt and embarrassment for children and parents alike. The report concludes that the government must do more to combat the exclusion and stigma caused by the costs of schooling, for example through the provision of funding for school uniform grants and 'activity funds'.[123]

National targets and priorities

Much of the government's focus over the past eight years has been on raising overall standards. For primary schools, it has focused on increasing the proportion of their pupils who achieve the Key Stage 2 targets, and for secondary schools the focus has been on increasing the proportion who achieve 'five good GCSEs.' These goals were given prominence in the 1998 and 2000 Spending Review, which set out the government's priorities for spending. Interestingly, more recent reviews have indicated a shift in priorities: the 2002 Spending Review included a new target on school attendance, while the current round of agreements, introduced in Spending Review 2004, marked a significant change, with a new set of targets to 'Safeguard children and young people, improve their life outcomes and general well-being, and break cycles of deprivation.'[124] Specific objectives include reducing the number of children living in households without paid work, reducing the under-18 conception rate, and reducing child obesity.

Very importantly from a life chances perspective, Spending Review 2004 introduced two education related inequality targets for DfES. The first addresses children's communication, social and emotional development at the end of the Foundation Stage (age five), and is to reduce inequalities between the level of development achieved by children in the 20 per cent most disadvantaged areas and the rest of England by 2008. The second is focused on looked after children and their performance at Key Stage 2 (end of primary school) and Key Stage 4 (end of secondary school) relative to their peers. However, although there are a number of floor targets, there are no inequality targets in relation to the wider schools population at Key Stages 1-4. Significant scope remains, therefore, for changes in the key PSA targets relating to schools to incorporate a higher profile for education inequality.

Inequality in post-16 pathways

2.5.1 Introduction

Social divisions exist in the pathways followed by young people after the end of compulsory education, with clear class differentials in entry to further and higher education, in degree completion, and in the types of institution and courses to which young people from different social backgrounds apply. Inequalities in post-school education are the culmination of inequalities throughout the early years and period of compulsory schooling, and have profound implications for their life chances. University graduates continue to enjoy significantly better prospects for employment and earnings in the labour market than non-graduates, with the highest returns being reaped disproportionately by those from privileged family backgrounds.[125] What is most worrying from a life chances perspective, however, is the high risk of negative outcomes in later life faced by young people who leave school early but do not enter employment or training, and it is on the life chances of this group that we focus particularly here.

2.5.2 The transition to further and higher education

- Although there has been some improvement in the last thirty years in the relative chances of young people from low income families staying on in full-time education after the end of compulsory schooling,[126] clear class differentials remain.

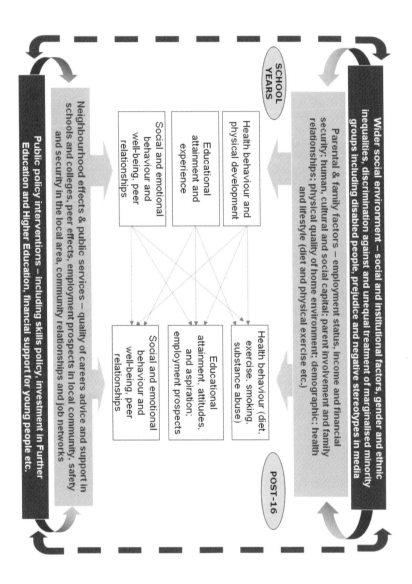

Figure 14
The life chances framework post-16.

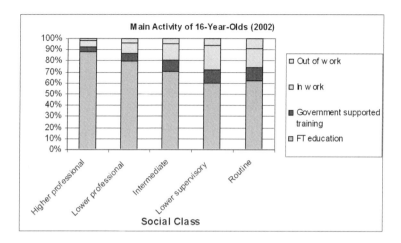

Figure 15
Main Activity of 16-year-olds (2002). *Source: DfES 2004.*

- In 2002, young people aged 16-19 from higher professional backgrounds were almost 1.5 times more likely to be in full-time education (87 per cent) than young people whose parents were in lower supervisory/routine manual occupations (60 per cent) (see Figure 15).

- Young people from minority ethnic groups are more likely on average to participate in full-time education after 16 than their white counterparts: the staying-on rate for white 16 year olds is 70 per cent, compared to 91 per cent for young people of Indian descent, 76 per cent for young people of Pakistani descent, 77 per cent for young people of Bangladeshi descent and 83 per cent for Black young people (see Figure 15).

- The proportion of 16, 17 and 18 year olds who are not in education, employment or training (NEET) has barely increased since the mid 1990s despite significant increases in overall employment rates during this period.

Socio-economic group	Percentage of all NEET at 16 in 2000*
Professional/managerial	7.5
Skilled non-manual	12.1
Skilled Manual	11.0
Semi/unskilled manual	13.1
No work/unclassified	56.4

Table 3
Percentage of 16 year olds not in education, employment or training (NEET) in 2000 by socio-economic group. Note: Data for young people who finished compulsory education in summer 2000.

- At the end of 2003, an estimated 9.0 per cent of 16-18 year olds were NEET, the same figure as for the end of 1994[127] (although more recent data suggests a slight fall from this level).[128]

- As shown in Table 3, the proportion of young people who are NEET at 16 is much higher amongst manual social class groups than non-manual groups.

- Young people who are NEET at 16 are more likely to come from workless households, to have parents with low or no educational qualifications, and to live in social rented housing. They are also three times more likely to have been excluded from school and twice as likely to have caring responsibilities.

- Perhaps surprisingly, a young person's qualification level at GCSE is not a good predictor of NEET status, and neither is the level of aspiration of the young person or their parents markedly different for the NEET group from those who enter work without training.[129]

Early school leaving is troubling from a life chances perspective because it is likely to have adverse effects upon young people's economic chances in later life. In particular, the consequences of early school leaving will be especially serious for those young people who become unemployed once they have left school. Young people aged 16-18 who are not in education, employment or training (NEET) are at a much higher risk of experiencing poor adult outcomes and perpetuating the cycle of disadvantage when they become parents in their turn.

2.5.3 Explaining the social divide in post-16 pathways

A key factor affecting individual decisions about whether or not to stay on at school is obviously whether or not pupils attain the required qualifications to be eligible for admission (though which comes first is an open question, since the decision to leave school early may undermine motivation and so lead to underperformance in examinations at 16; conversely, low attainment may force someone to leave school early if they fail to gain the necessary qualifications to continue in full-time education).

But academic factors can only explain part of class differences in post-16 pathways. While the attainment of formal qualifications is hugely important – because young people do not have the option to continue if they fail to meet the entry requirements – we also need to look at processes of selection and *self*-selection: at an individual level, this means looking at rates of application and the decisions made by young people age 16 to 18 about courses and institutions; at an institutional level, it means looking at the fairness and transparency of admissions procedures, and the efforts made by institutions of further and higher education to encourage and promote fair access.

At the level of individual decisions and behaviour, what matters besides attainment is that young people want – and are able – to proceed into further and higher education. Research reveals that even with the same academic performance, students from lower socio-economic backgrounds are less likely to take up A-level courses than their more privileged peers.[130] A common explanation given for this lower take-up of opportunities is that it reflects a lack – some say a 'poverty' – of aspiration and ambition on the part of young people from lower socio-economic backgrounds. This kind of view fails to take into account the wider range of constraints (financial, social and psychological) faced by young people from lower socio-economic backgrounds, which can be traced to the social environment in which they live and grow up.

Another common view is that it betrays a less rational approach to decision-making and a failure properly to comprehend the future benefits and economic returns to education.[131] An alternative explanation is given by John Goldthorpe, who stresses that the choices of low-income students represent a rational response to unequal risk.[132] As Goldthorpe emphasises, there is wide variation in the context in which young people make decisions. Parental earning curves of different social classes are at their most divergent around the time when their children leave school, and it is at this time when 'the question of opportunity costs first arises'.[133]

Those who are brought up in a family where more education is highly valued, and with the expectation that they will go to university, will tend to value education positively. Young people's views are also likely to be shaped by their peer group and by the schools they attend: in schools with a strong academic ethos, for example, (which may well be a reflection of parents' priorities), there may be considerable pressure towards university participation. Schools also provide information about the available courses and institutions and advice on qualifications relevant to specific careers, as well as more practical help with filling in application forms, through dedicated careers advisors or in specific careers lessons.[134] One important issue to be addressed is the relevance of the advice given to young people, especially those who do not follow the conventional academic pathway from GCSEs to university via A-levels. In a recent study of young people's attitudes to higher education, careers advice was much more likely to be regarded as irrelevant by those with lower levels of academic attainment. Low-attaining young people tended to feel that careers advice was only targeted at 'high achievers'.[135] The study also suggests that young people who are interested in less mainstream careers find it difficult 'to get specific and appropriate advice because career advisors do not have connections with the full range of potential employers'.[136]

2.5.4 Public policy considerations

The government has taken action in recent years to target the group of approximately 200,000 young people aged 16-18 who are currently NEET. It has introduced educational subsidies for sixteen to eighteen years olds staying in post-compulsory education, in the form of the Educational Maintenance Allowance (EMA). Evaluations suggest that the EMA has increased both participation and retention in post-16 further education. With the introduction of EMAs, initial participation rates were 4.5 per cent higher, and a year later the participation rates were 6.4 per cent higher, suggesting that the grant works to prevent initial participants from dropping out at a later stage.[137] The IFS estimates that just over half of the individuals who stayed in education would otherwise have been inactive (NEETs) rather than in work. Critically, the effect of the EMA grant was found to be greatest on children from the poorest socio-economic backgrounds.[138]

The Connexions service was launched in 2001, bringing together all the careers services given to young people by public, voluntary and private sector groups. Performance data for the Connexions service demonstrates some success for the policy: in all local areas where Connexions services became operational in or before November 2002, the proportion of 16 to 18 year olds not in employment, education or training reduced from 9 per cent in 2002 to 7.7 per cent in 2004. In some areas a more significant reduction, of up to 4 per cent, was achieved.139 Given that the proportion of young people not in education, employment or training remained broadly level from the 1990s, the modest success demonstrated by Connexions implies that targeted interventions of this type, providing information and advice for young people, can make a positive impact on levels of activity and participation for this age group.[140]

More remains to be done, however, to assist those whom education currently fails. Research suggests that there is considerable variation in the quantity and quality of 'next steps' advice between schools.141 It is therefore important that careers services in schools and colleges, as well as external careers services such as Connexions, are equipped to give information and advice on the full range of options available to young people, whether in further or higher education or in employment. It may also be necessary to counter the bias towards the traditional route into higher education (GCSEs, followed by A-levels and university) by making sure that school-leavers are properly informed about the options for returning to study after entering the labour market.

Wider inequalities in society

2.6.1 Introduction

Our analysis thus far has focused on successive stages of children's development from the start of life through the early and school years, and into early adulthood. In this section, we focus on the wider inequalities in society which affect people's life chances and which shape their experience of poverty and low income. In the first part we review child and family poverty. In the second part, we focus on inequalities of income and wealth. In the final part, we look at broader social inequalities relating to gender, ethnicity and disability.

2.6.2 The impact of poverty on children's life chances

Parts 2.2 to 2.5 have repeatedly shown that children who are born into low income families have a much higher risk of suffering poor outcomes – in their physical, intellectual and social development in early childhood; in their educational attainment and the acquisition of social skills and wide social networks in later childhood; and in terms of their income, employment and a range of other outcomes in adulthood. The experience of poverty undermines children's chances to flourish and thrive, and to grow up to live fulfilling and rewarding lives. This is why the Commission defines 'poverty' as the inability, due to lack of resources, to participate in society and to enjoy a standard of living consistent with human dignity and social decency, and why we define *child poverty* as the inability to enjoy the kind of childhood taken for granted in the wider society, due to lack of resources.

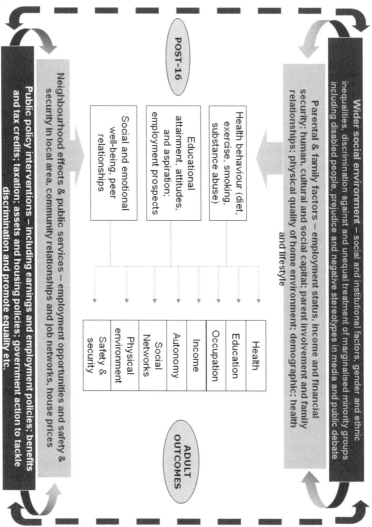

Figure 16

The life chances framework from post-16 into adulthood.

60 per cent of 2003/04 median income	BHC	AHC
Family net income per week in 2003/04 prices		
Couple no children	£201	£178
Single no children	£123	£98
Couple 2 children aged 5 and 11	£294	£262
Single 2 children aged 5 and 11	£216	£182

Table 4
Relative poverty line before housing costs and after housing costs,
Great Britain 2003/04. Source: HBAI 2003/04, Table C. Note: income
is equivalised, and is 'disposable' income, i.e. after direct taxes and
benefits.

Many people's intuitive understanding of poverty is one of
absolute penury. However, the standard measure of poverty in
the UK is relative, with a household considered to be poor if its
income is less than 60 per cent of the median for a household of
that type. Table 4 shows the poverty threshold on this measure,
before and after housing costs, for different family types.
Relative poverty is important because when people's income
falls too far below the average they become unable to do the
things that most people take for granted. If we were using a
measure of what would have been considered poverty in the
19th Century, there would be almost no measured poverty in
Britain today. Yet many people in contemporary Britain are
unable to live the kind of lives that most people take for granted
because of lack of financial resources.

Progress in tackling child and family poverty in recent years

- In 2003/04 there were 2.6 million children living in households below the poverty line of 60 per cent of contemporary
  median income before housing costs, and 3.5 million children
  using the after housing costs measure (Table 5).

Narrowing the Gap

	Relative poverty BHC (<60 percent contemporary median household income)[143]		Relative poverty AHC (<60 percent contemporary median household income)	
	% children	no. of children (millions)	% children	no. of children (millions)
1996/1997	25	3.2	33	4.2
1997/1998	25	3.1	32	4.1
1998/1999	24	3.1	33	4.1
1999/2000	23	3.0	32	4.1
2000/2001	21	2.7	30	3.8
2001/2002	21	2.6	30	3.7
2002/2003	21	2.6	28	3.6
2003/2004	21	2.6	28	3.5

Table 5
Relative child poverty rates in Great Britain1996/97 – 2003/04, before and after housing costs[142] Source: HBAI 2003/04, Opportunity For All indicators

- Just over one fifth (21 per cent) of children in Great Britain live in relative poverty today on the BHC measure, as compared to over one quarter (28 per cent) on the AHC measure.

There has been significant progress in tackling child poverty since 1996/97, with some 600,000 fewer children now living in relative poverty than at the beginning of this period on the government's central measure of income before housing costs. However, progress appears to have stalled in the last few years. Whilst the tide has been turned on the very high levels of poverty Labour inherited in 1997, overall poverty levels are still high and the scale of the challenge to halve child poverty by 2010 and abolish it by 2020 remains considerable.

116

The government has introduced a new measure of poverty against which it will judge progress towards the 2010 and 2020 targets. This has three components: a fixed value low income measure (60 per cent of median income in 1998/99), a relative low income measure (60 per cent of contemporary median household income), and a combination of below 70 per cent of relative contemporary low income and material deprivation (which is still being developed).

Whilst we do not focus on measurement issues in this report, it is worth making three brief points. Firstly, the government is now defining 'eradication' of child poverty as having poverty rates that are amongst the best in Europe. This has prompted criticism from some quarters that it represents a retreat and loss of ambition. However, it would never have been possible to totally eradicate relative poverty, as there will always be some individuals with temporarily low incomes. The goal of achieving child poverty rates in Britain that are amongst the best in Europe is still both extremely important and ambitious. It would mean dramatically reducing child poverty rates from their current level of 21 per cent to around five per cent, and does not in practice represent a significant retreat from its original goal.

Secondly, we think the inclusion of a material deprivation indicator, to capture the reality of living standards for those living in poverty, is an important innovation. However, thirdly, we are concerned that the government is intending to focus exclusively on income measures which are reported before housing costs, as many low income families have little choice over this important aspect of their budget. This issue makes a particular difference to the geographical distribution of measured poverty. As a minimum, we believe that the government should, as promised, continue to report income measures after housing costs so that this issue can be monitored effectively.

The risk of poverty for different groups

So who is poor in Great Britain today? Table 6 presents three sets of information for the child population considered in terms of various different characteristics. First it shows the proportion of the total child population, poor and non-poor, in each category. Second it shows what proportion of all the children who are living in poverty belong to each category. The final column indicates the proportion of children in each category who are living in poverty. This can be considered as their *risk* of poverty.

It is important to bear in mind that there will be significant variation in poverty rates within many categories. Not all people living in Inner London will be at equal risk of poverty, nor all people of Pakistani or Bangladeshi descent. Categories may also overlap in important ways, for example, in the interface between gender and ethnicity. Of course, information about the incidence or risk of poverty amongst different groups is only the first part of the story; it does not in itself tell us about the causes of poverty, although it suggests a number of avenues of inquiry. In particular, it draws attention to the close associations between poverty and wider inequalities of various kinds, and with cross-cutting divisions in society such as race and disability, and indicates the need for specific policies to address problems faced by particular groups. The issues raised by these social divisions are discussed in the final section below.

- The risk of poverty is particularly high for children in households without paid work, at 55 per cent against 21 per cent for the child population as a whole.

- Nonetheless, more than half of all child poverty (54 per cent) occurs in households where at least one parent is doing some paid work. Paid work is extremely important but is not a panacea for poverty.

- There is a clear gradient where larger families are more at risk of poverty. Families with four or more children are more than twice as likely to have low income as families with one or two children.

- The presence of a disabled adult in the family increases the risk of child poverty from 19 to 30 per cent.

- The risk of poverty among different ethnic groups is very varied, but overall all minority groups fare worse than white families. The risk of poverty among Pakistani and Bangladeshi families is particularly severe at 61 per cent.

- Poverty is unevenly distributed across different regions, with a particular concentration in Inner London, and a noticeable North/South divide. As noted, the regional distribution of poverty is affected by the use of Before Housing Cost figures.

2.6.3 Inequalities of income and wealth

As we discuss in section 2.6.8, poverty is nested within inequalities of various kinds, including cross-cutting social divisions such as gender, ethnicity and disability. But it is particularly closely associated with inequalities of income and wealth. Although they are not the same, relative poverty and inequality are closely connected, and the forces which lead to inequalities shape the context in which poverty is created and determine its volume and nature.

While we are principally concerned about income inequality because of its effect on the life chances of children in lower income families, it is important to emphasise that income inequalities have effects throughout society. There is a growing body of evidence demonstrating people in the middle of the earnings distribution doing systematically worse across a range of 'life chances' dimensions, than people at the top, just as people at the bottom do systematically worse than people in the middle. Moreover, research suggests that the overall quality of social relations in a society is adversely affected by wide inequalities.[144] Income inequalities are not just a matter of concern for people living in poverty.

Narrowing the Gap

	Proportion of all children in each group %	Proportion of poor children in each group %	Risk of poverty for children in each group %
Economic status and family type			
Lone parent:	24	38	32
of which			
in full-time work	5	1	6
in part-time work	6	6	18
not in paid work	13	31	49
Couple with children:	76	62	17
of which			
self-employed	11	12	23
both in full-time work	12	1	2
one in full-time work, one in part-time work	23	4	3
one in full-time work, one not working	19	14	16
one or more in part-time work	5	11	48
both not in paid work	7	20	63
Economic status of household			
All adults in work	56	20	7
At least one in work, but not all	27	34	26
Households without paid work	17	46	55
Number of children in family			
One	24	19	16
Two	44	36	17
Three	22	25	24
Four or more	10	20	41
Disability			
No disabled adults	83	75	19
1 or more disabled adults	17	25	30
No disabled children	90	89	20
1 or more disabled children	10	11	22
of which			
no disabled adults in family	7	6	19
1 or more disabled adults in family	4	5	29
All children	12.5m	2.6m	21%

	Proportion of all children in each group %	Proportion of poor children in each group %	Risk of poverty for children in each group %
Ethnic group			
White	88	76	18
Mixed	1	1	30
Asian or Asian British	6	14	49
of which			
Indian	2	4	36
Pakistani/Bangladeshi	3	9	61
Black or Black British	3	6	35
Chinese or other ethnic group	2	3	35
Geographical disaggregation			
England	87	86	20
of which			
North East	4	5	25
North West and Merseyside	12	14	23
Yorkshire and the Humber	9	10	23
East Midlands	7	7	20
West Midlands	10	12	26
Eastern	9	8	17
London	13	17	27
of which			
Inner	5	8	36
Outer	8	9	22
South East	14	7	11
South West	8	6	16
Scotland	8	9	22
Wales	5	5	21
All children	12.5m	2.6m	21%

Table 6 (left and above): The child population, children living in relative poverty (<60 per cent median household income before housing costs), and relative poverty rates for different groups in Great Britain, 2003/04. *Source: HBAI 2003/04.Note: poverty is measured here as less than 60 per cent of contemporary median equivalised income before housing costs, consistent with the government's measure of relative poverty. Note: work means paid work in this table.*

Inequalities in the distribution of income

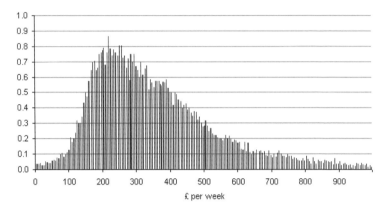

Figure 17

Distribution of weekly household income[1], 2002/03, Great Britain.

1: Number of individuals (millions). Equivalised household disposable income before housing costs (in £5 bands). *Source: Households Below Average Income, Department for Work and Pensions.*

Figure 17 demonstrates the considerable inequality that exists in the distribution of weekly household income.145 It shows that there is a greater concentration of people at the bottom end of the income spectrum, with half the population having household disposable incomes of less than £325 per week146. In 2002/03, almost two-thirds of the population had incomes below the national *average* of £396 per week. The distribution is skewed by a long tail of people on high incomes: 1.6 million individuals live in households with more than £1,000 per week but these are not shown in the figure. In terms of changes in the distribution of income over time, Figure 18 shows how the gradual decrease in inequality in the 1970s was reversed during the early 1980s, with the income of the top ten per cent of households rising sharply compared to the median and the bottom ten per cent the for the rest of the decade.

United Kingdom/Great Britain
£ per week

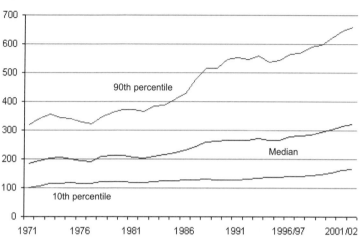

Figure 18
Distribution of real[1] disposable household income[2,3]

1: Data adjusted to 2002/03 prices using the Retail Prices Index less local taxes.
2: Equivalised household disposable income before housing costs.
Source: Institute for Fiscal Studies from Family Expenditure Survey; Households Below Average Income, Department for Work and Pensions.

During the 1980s, the incomes of richer individuals grew faster than those of poorer individuals throughout the income distribution. This pattern can be seen in Table 7, which shows the share of total income received by each quintile of households. Each quintile contains 20 per cent of all households, with the bottom quintile containing the 20 per cent with the lowest incomes. The table shows how the impact of taxes and benefits changes this pattern.

	Original income			Gross income			Disposable income			Post-tax income		
Quintile	1978	96-7	03-4	1978	96-7	03-4	1978	96-7	03-4	1978	96-7	03-4
Bottom	3	2	3	9	7	7	10	8	8	10	7	7
2nd	10	7	7	13	11	11	14	12	12	14	11	12
3rd	18	15	15	18	16	16	18	16	17	18	16	16
4th	26	25	24	23	23	22	23	23	22	23	22	22
Top	43	51	51	37	44	44	35	42	42	36	44	44

Table 7
Percentage shares of household income, by income quintile, 1978 – 2003/04. *Source: ONS. Note 1: figures do not all sum to 100 due to rounding. Note 2: Original income is before government intervention, and is principally from employment, self employment and investments. Gross income includes cash benefits such as child benefit and state pensions. Disposable income incorporates the effect of direct taxes such as income tax and employee National Insurance Contributions. Post tax income incorporates the effect of indirect taxes such as VAT and duties.*

- Between 1978 and 1996-7 the top 20 per cent of households increased their share of original income from 43 to 51 per cent, at the expense of all other quintiles.

- Over the same period the impact of taxes and benefits became less progressive. In 1978 the tax and benefit system increased the income share of the bottom 20 per cent of households from three to ten per cent. By 1996-7 it increased it only from two to seven per cent.

- Between 1996/97 and 2002/03, income growth has been much more evenly spread across the whole of the income distribution, with exceptions only at the very top and bottom of the distribution.

Public policy has a powerful impact on household incomes. Our capacity to secure employment and earn an income is strongly affected by our skills and other aspects of our personal development, which in turn are influenced by major public services such as health and education. The supply of and demand for labour, and the rewards to work, are shaped by economic policies. Government also plays a major role in redistributing income between different households via benefits, taxes and public services. In addition, it has a potentially powerful role to play in influencing social norms which are crucial in determining wage dispersion and the distribution of income.

Since 1997 the government has introduced a range of policies on employment and earnings, on benefits, tax credits, and taxation that have enabled it to prevent further increases in income inequality compared to what would have occurred had the 1996 tax and benefits system simply been annually uprated. However, despite the decidedly redistributive effect of these measures, it remains the case that the government has only managed to contain income inequality and has not yet managed to reverse the trend.[147]

2.6.4 Income from Earnings

For the great majority of children in the UK, parental earnings from employment are the primary source of household income. Earnings are central to both poverty and inequality, and therefore to life chances. Earnings before taxes and benefits are sometimes described as 'original income', in the sense that they come before the intervention of government. However, government affects original income in many ways. It is a central purpose of the education system to develop in young people the capacities which enable them to earn an income later in life. Other public services, from early years services to healthcare to housing, are similarly important even if they do not have the same explicit aim. If some groups systematically experience poor outcomes in terms of their development of skills and capacities, then they will in turn be disadvantaged in the labour market. Improving the basic life chances of children through improving public services for the disadvantaged, as well as directly addressing low income, is thus central to achieving our long-term ambition for the abolition of child poverty and the creation of a less divided society.

Another fundamental way in which the government affects earnings is via its management of the economy. Since the mid 1990s, the UK has enjoyed an exceptionally long period of low inflation and steady growth in output. Over the same period, overall unemployment has fallen to near its all-time historic low; and overall employment has risen to near its historic high, standing at approximately 75 per cent in mid 2005. However, the comparable figures for disadvantaged groups are much more challenging even where their employment rates have been moving in the right direction in recent years. We are some way from 'full employment' if this is defined as 'everyone who wants to work can quickly find a job [and] no groups are excluded from the labour market'[148]. Achieving the government's ambition of an overall employment rate of 80 per cent would mean an additional 2.5 million people finding work, compared to approximately two million who did so between mid 1997 and mid 2005. This is clearly an extremely ambitious goal which will require consistent political focus over an extended period.

In addition to policies to encourage a benign overall economic environment, the government has implemented a number of reforms targeted specifically at unemployed and 'workless' people more generally, most notably the New Deals and the Jobcentre Plus reforms.[149] Both have been subject to wide-ranging evaluation, the general message of which has been that the New Deals have had modest success, and represent relatively good value for money in terms of getting people into work.[150] The integrated Jobcentre Plus service, meanwhile, has been monitored continuously since its inception in 2001, and internal and external evaluations show that progress has been made, with growing evidence that the integrated services are helping more lone parents and people with health conditions and disabilities into work – though difficulties remain with regard to a work-focused approach for people with health conditions and disabilities, and carers.[151]

Where there has been more concern is over the durability of these jobs and the opportunities for progression that they offer, which has led some to question the emphasis on work over training that is more or less explicit in policies such as the New Deals and Jobcentre Plus. We might ask therefore whether a 'work first' approach to employment is the most appropriate approach to take, and whether a better approach would be to concentrate on developing the capacities of the individual.

2.6.5 Income from Benefits and Tax Credits

Cash benefits and tax credits make up more than half of the gross income of the fifth of families with children who have the lowest incomes.[152] As this is the group in which child poverty is largely concentrated, changes in benefits and tax credits thus have a highly significant impact on child poverty. Because benefits and tax credits make up a progressively lower share of household income as incomes rise, they also significantly reduce overall household income inequality.[153]

Child Benefit and Child Tax Credit can be described as the twin foundations of welfare for low income children. Child Benefit, designed to help all families with children with the direct costs of children, is currently received by approximately seven million families and in 2003/04 accounted for £9.4 billion of expenditure. Child Tax Credit was introduced to give particular help to low income families, though some entitlement is extended to most families, with the intention of reducing the stigma of claiming it. Some element of Child Tax Credit is currently received by around 6 million families, which in 2003/04 accounted for £8.8 billion of expenditure.[154] The two benefits thus account for similar shares of total government expenditure, though recent assessments suggest that Child Tax Credit may now be overtaking Child Benefit in this regard.[155]

Another way of considering the balance between the two benefits is via their importance at the family level. This is much more complex, because whilst Child Benefit is a universal, non-contributory benefit, Child Tax Credit is means tested and the amount received thus depends both on family income and on take-up. However, it is possible to give some illustrative examples for families who are out of work or with low earnings in 2005/06:[156]

- A lone parent with one non-disabled child over the age of one, and full entitlement to both the family and per child element of the tax credit, will receive £17.00 per week in Child Benefit and £42.98 per week in Child Tax Credit.

- A two parent family with two non-disabled children, one of six months and another over the age of one, and full entitlement to both the family and per child element of the tax credit, will receive £28.40 per week in Child Benefit and £85.96 per week in Child Tax Credit.[157]

It is clear that for families with full entitlement, Child Tax Credit makes up a far higher proportion of their income than Child Benefit. Child Benefit has increased from £11.05 per week for the only or eldest child and £9.00 for other children in 1997/98, to £17.00 for the only or eldest child and £11.40 for other children in 2005/06. However, the only year in this period when it was increased by more than inflation was 1999, when it jumped from £11.45 to £14.40 for the first child. Significant extra resources have been made available to support low income households, but these have otherwise come through the new tax credits.

2.6.6 Taxation

Taxation plays a number of key roles in relation to child poverty and life chances. It is the principal source of funds for the public services and benefits that are the key tools to combat poverty and improve opportunities for disadvantaged children. In addition, taxation also affects household incomes more immediately. In 2003/04 the lowest income fifth of nonretired households paid 39 per cent of their gross income in taxes, whereas the highest income fifth paid 35 per cent.∎

As well as requiring a taxation regime that raises the necessary public funds, we are thus also interested in reforms to taxation that would reduce the burden on people on low incomes and reduce the overall level of income inequality. The overall impact of taxation in the UK is in fact slightly regressive, adding to the overall inequality of incomes. However, this is the result of two opposing forces. The principal direct taxes – income tax and National Insurance Contributions – are progressive, taking a bigger share of higher incomes and reducing overall inequality. However, the total impact of the myriad of indirect taxes – principally VAT and various duties – is even more strongly regressive, taking a bigger share of lower incomes and slightly outweighing the impact of direct taxes on overall inequality. Whilst taxation has not been a principal focus of the Commission on Life Chances and Child Poverty, we share the ambition of the earlier Fabian Commission on Taxation and Citizenship to make the overall impact of taxation more progressive in the UK.

2.6.7 Assets

Wealth is another resource which is fundamental to life chances, and it is even more unevenly distributed than income.159 Whereas the 20 per cent of households with the highest incomes accounted for 44 per cent of all post tax income in 2003-4, the wealthiest ten per cent of the population accounted for 56 per cent of all marketable wealth in 2002.160 By contrast half the entire UK population shared just six per cent of such wealth in the same year. The 1980s did not see an explosion in wealth inequality in the same way as income; but by the 1990s the widening gap in disposable income had begun to translate itself into inequalities in accumulated wealth, with the shift in the distribution of wealth towards the top one per cent continuing up

	1%	2%	3-5%	6-10%	11-25%	26-50%	51-100%
1979	20	6	11	13	22	20	8
1997	22	8	13	11	21	18	7
2002	24	7	13	13	18	20	6

Table 8:
Proportion of all marketable wealth owned, by percentiles of adult population. *Source: HM Revenue & Customs 2004. Note: 2002 figures are provisional.*

---

to 2002 (the latest period at the time of writing for which data was available).

Over the course of the twentieth century the share of wealth held by the very wealthiest one per cent of the population declined very significantly, from around 70 per cent in 1911, to around 40 per cent in 1960, and finally down to below 20 per cent in the late 1980s. However since this time the share of this top one per cent of wealth owners has begun to increase again, from 17 per cent in 1991 to 24 per cent in 2004. Over the same period the share of wealth held by everyone outside the wealthiest ten per cent declined from 53 per cent to 44 per cent. Wealth is once again concentrating in fewer hands.

Today, around a third of the population has little or no accessible savings.[161] This is worrying because the possession of even modest amounts of wealth can be an important protective factor for low income families, for example when earnings from employment are interrupted or unexpected costs are incurred. Although it does not provide a current flow of income, having ownership of marketable assets such as housing is an important source of financial security (against which loans, for example, can be secured), while selling or re-mortgaging a property allows for a release of income in the future. This kind of security helps protect against unexpected events that affect the regular flow of income. Large concentrations of wealth, meanwhile, allow families to transmit advantages in life chances to their children via privileged access to housing, education, and opportunities to take risks such as starting a business.

Since 1997 the government has taken important steps to establish asset based welfare as a new element of the welfare state, particularly via the Child Trust Fund and the Savings Gateway. These policies are particularly focused on the 'asset poor' and are to be welcomed as an addition to policies designed to tackle low incomes. However, as with income, there has been relatively little focus or progress in relation to asset inequality, as opposed to asset poverty. An important issue that this report does not address specifically is the position of those with very high incomes and very large amounts of wealth. The top one per cent of both earners and asset owners appear to be pulling ahead of the rest of the population at a rapid rate,[162] and it will be important to understand what effects this is likely to have on life chances.

Inheritance Tax has not been significantly reformed since 1997. The rate has not been changed, and nor has the basic structure. The threshold has gone up by more than inflation but less than the rate of overall growth in either earnings or wealth. It remains relatively easy to avoid, especially for the very wealthy who can both afford good financial advice about avoidance mechanisms, and more securely give away the bulk of their assets more than seven years before their death.

Inheritance Tax can more accurately be described as an estates tax. A £500,000 estate is currently taxed in the same way whether it is bequeathed to a single individual or divided between 50 people. In addition, the nature and number of the legatees are irrelevant. On the one hand, this means that there is no fiscal incentive for people to disperse their wealth. On the other hand, the inheritance is affected by tax in the same way regardless of whether the inheritor is wealthy or poor. There are grounds, therefore, for arguing in line with the Fabian Commission on Taxation and Citizenship that the burden of inheritance taxation should be shifted from the estate to the recipients.

2.6.8 Wider social divisions and inequalities

People's life chances are not only related to their socio-economic status, but are also closely associated with social divisions of various kinds. In particular, there are strong links between ethnic status, disability, and gender, and people's outcomes in later life. These faultlines within society not only exacerbate the risk of poverty for many people, and influence the lived experience of poverty for these groups, but also constitute inequalities in their own right, which structure life chances for many more.

Here, we review the evidence of systematic inequalities for particular social groups and examine the main causes of these outcomes, noting in particular the extent to which the unequal treatment reflects discrimination and prejudice. In the final section, we review progress in tackling these kinds of social inequalities at a policy level. A key argument here is that discrimination against people in poverty (at both an individual and institutional level) needs to be recognised and tackled through policies, in the same way as discrimination on the grounds of gender or race or disability.

Gender inequality and women's poverty

Women's poverty is an important issue in its own right, as well as having implications for the success of the government's child poverty strategy.[163] Moreover, tackling gender inequalities is crucial, because children themselves grow up in a gendered world, which shapes their opportunities and outcomes in different ways.

Children's experience of poverty is both shaped by, and linked to, women's poverty. The Women's Budget Group highlights the close connections between women's poverty and children's poverty. As the main managers of family income, mothers frequently go without basic items such as food and clothing themselves in order to shield their children from the harsh effects of poverty.164 The struggle to make ends meet on a very low income also means that women are exposed to high levels of stress and anxiety, which may affect their physical and mental health.[165] As discussed above, mothers and pregnant women on low income report feeling a lack of control over their lives, which helps explain their often fatalistic attitudes to diet, smoking and other health-related behaviours.[166] Women on low incomes may also experience feelings of guilt and inadequacy due to the pressure of trying to provide materially for their children and of trying to protect them from the stigmatising effects of being poor and of wearing the 'wrong' clothes.[167]

- Women are at greater risk of living in poverty than men: according to the Department for Work and Pensions (2004), 21 per cent of women live in poverty, compared to 19 per cent of men.[168] But these figures, based on Households Below Average Income statistics, actually obscure the real extent of women's vulnerability to poverty, because they cannot take account of the unfair distribution of resources within households.

- Women are approximately 5 per cent more likely to be in households below the poverty line than men, and are at greater risk of experiencing persistent low income.[169]

Women's greater vulnerability to poverty is due in part to the difficulties of combining work and caring responsibilities. As well as continuing to have primary responsibility for children's welfare in the majority of households, women are far more likely than men to be carers of elderly relatives, which affects their capacity to undertake paid work and so increases their risk of living below the poverty line. Women are also more exposed to poverty because they are more likely to be lone parents (over 90 per cent of lone parents are women) and so face greater obstacles to combining work and childcare responsibilities.[170] For women in couples, the continued existence of a gendered division of labour within the home means that women are more likely to lack economic independence from their partners and less likely to be able to accrue savings that can protect against poverty in the event of sudden loss of income.

The nature of opportunities for all is also gendered in our society. For younger birth cohorts, the gap between men's and women's education and training has been eroded, with young women today developing human capital in many ways superior to that of their male counterparts. Much of the gender gap in qualifications and human capital in the past was due to prevailing attitudes and expectations about the role of men and women in society, as well as discrimination in the education system and at home which affected the importance placed on girls' schooling as compared to boys'.

- The gap in women's and men's education and skills has narrowed in recent decades. At school level, girls' average educational attainment is now higher than boys'.

- But despite the fact that girls are outperforming boys in school, gender inequalities re-emerge once men and women leave full-time education. Three years after graduating, female graduates earn 15 per cent less, on average, than their male counterparts.[171]

- The most recent figures, published by the Office of National Statistics, show that the gender pay gap for full-time workers is 18 per cent, and the gap between part-time women workers and full-time male workers is 40 per cent.[172] In 2004, men had average gross weekly earnings of £525, as compared to £396 for women.[173]

- Jobs which are disproportionately done by women (such as childcare, catering and cleaning) continue to be less well-paid than those in other sectors. And women are more likely than men to be in low-paid, part-time employment.[174]

At the heart of lifetime differences in individual income is the 'gendered division of labour' – i.e. the fact that women and men tend to do different types of work both within and outside the home.175 The Women and Work Commission identifies three main factors sustaining the gender pay gap: part-time working, occupational segregation and women's labour market issues, such as childcare, which act as barriers to women's chances of entering and progressing in the workplace. Although discrimination against women in the labour market has declined over the last thirty years, recent research by the Policy Studies Institute concludes that it was still an important cause of the gender pay gap in the 1990s, accounting for 46 per cent of the pay gap between males and females in full-time employment.[176]

Furthermore, the benefits system may also play a role in encouraging traditional gender roles, for example through the 'under-valuing of caring, the reflection of gender-related labour market inequalities in benefit entitlement, and the influence of the idea of the male as the norm on welfare provision'.[177]

The continuing inequalities in men's and women's income and opportunities point to the need for a gendered employment strategy, as well as reform to the benefit system (including parental leave arrangements and pension provision), as part of a broader strategy to combat gender inequalities. A gendered employment strategy needs to be explicitly targeted towards: improving access to quality part-time employment; ending the occupational segregation that so often relegates women to low-paid sectors; and addressing the various practical obstacles that inhibit women's entry or re-entry into the labour market, once they have had children, as discussed in section 2.3.3. The government has pledged to introduce a public sector duty to promote gender equality by December 2006, which should encourage public authorities to review pay systems. It has also signalled its commitment to addressing the gender pay gap, through the appointment of the Women and Work Commission in September 2004 to look at the 'wide-ranging influences on the gender pay gap' and to make recommendations on closing it, to ensure a 'fair deal in the labour market'.[178] But it remains to be seen whether the government will heed the recommendations of the Women and Work Commission,[179] especially given that previous groups set up to look at the issue have not always been met with concerted action at a policy level.

Ethnic Inequalities

The picture of ethnic inequality in the UK is particularly complex. It is important to remember that just as the incidence of poverty, educational underachievement and unemployment varies widely amongst members of the white British community, there is also wide variation in outcomes among members of Black and minority ethnic British communities, with a complex pattern of outcomes between and within different Black and minority ethnic groups. Young people's chances of achieving good educational and employment outcomes, along with their other life chances, are by no means determined by their ethnicity, but depend on a wide range of individual, parental and family variables, as well as being affected by policy and societal factors. But the high incidence of poverty amongst certain ethnic minority groups, as well as the fact that they are at such a high risk of suffering poor outcomes in other areas of life (including education and the labour market) should alert us to a source of continuing and deep-rooted inequality in British society.

- Pakistani and Bangladeshi children are at particularly high risk of growing up in poverty, with a poverty rate of 61 per cent, nearly three times the average.[180]

- Over 30 per cent of Pakistani and Black pupils are eligible for free school meals, as are over 50 per cent of Bangladeshi, Gypsy/Roma and pupils of Travellers of Irish heritage, as compared to just 14 per cent of White pupils.[181]

The high risk of poverty amongst Pakistani and Bangladeshi communities is partly due to the high propensity of larger families amongst these groups. Pakistani and Bangladeshi families have an average of 4.7 and 4.2 people in a household, as compared to an average of 2.3 for white families.[182] Living in a large family (i.e. those with three or more children) increases the risk of growing up in poverty, though the risk of poverty amongst large families has gone down markedly since 1998/9.[183]

- Pupils of Chinese and Indian descent have the highest average attainment of five or more GCSEs, outperforming White pupils in this regard.[184]

- Pupils of Bangladeshi and Pakistani descent are more likely to achieve lower qualifications than their peers,[185] and to leave school without any qualifications.[186]

- Black Caribbean boys are at particularly high risk of being permanently excluded from school.[187]

Part of the explanation for the pattern of inequality in school outcomes may lie in the high prevalence of poverty amongst particular groups, as well as in the spatial concentration of certain ethnic minority groups in deprived areas. A recent synthesis of research for the Cabinet Office Strategy Unit shows that a complex interaction exists between socio-economic group, ethnicity and educational achievement.[188] The report concludes that socio-economic factors are paramount in affecting the educational attainment of certain minority ethnic groups, whilst recognising that these only tell a part of the story. Other factors that may affect the educational attainment of certain ethnic minority groups in schools include lack of English language fluency, racial abuse or harassment, lack of positive role models, unfamiliarity (amongst parents) with the workings of the British education system, and teaching based on unfamiliar cultural norms, histories and points of reference.[189]

The fact that Black pupils experience a dramatic decline in their performance relative to other groups, despite entering the school system with assessments that are generally in advance of the LEA average,[190] indicates that wider factors than socio-economic disadvantage must be considered in understanding and addressing their low average attainment. While low expectations and aspirations of parents or pupils themselves and of parental engagement in children's education have been cited as factors in lower attainment, there is little evidence that this is specifically related to ethnicity.[191] One possible explanation is that teachers' judgements and expectations of ability disadvantage particular ethnic groups,[192] though the extent to which low attainment can be attributed to low teacher expectation or differential treatment in the classroom is a matter of continuing controversy. David Gillborn argues that a 'myth of an African

Caribbean challenge' exists in British schools, whereby teachers see Black boys in particular as threatening their authority.[193] Deborah Youdell argues that African-Caribbean students develop a distinctive subculture *in order to resist* their differential treatment in schools, although a differential subculture could also originate outside of school processes, and may contribute to differential treatment of some minority ethnic pupils.[194] Andrew Pilkington, meanwhile, argues that 'at least in the latter stages of schooling, the behaviour of some African-Caribbean pupils is not only defined by teachers as deviant, but is in fact deviant'.[195] This suggests the existence of a cyclical relationship, whereby both differential treatment and 'bad' behaviour contribute to low average attainment for particular minority ethnic groups.

- In general terms, only 60 per cent of the working age Black and Minority Ethnic (BME) population are in work compared to 75 per cent of the working age population as a whole – a gap of 15 per cent.

- But the employment gap is much wider for some groups: Pakistani and Bangladeshi men are three times as likely to be unemployed as the population as a whole.

- Employment rates for women vary significantly across minority ethnic groups. For example, 72 per cent of White women are in employment, compared to just 25 per cent of Bangladeshi and Pakistani women, and 49 per cent of Black women of African origin.[196]

There is also evidence of continued discrimination and racism in the workplace. The effectiveness of anti-racist legislation and equal opportunities policies in workplaces in improving the lives of Black and minority ethnic people is examined in a recent review of existing research. It finds that changes to recruitment procedures have improved the employment prospects of minorities, but that there is still evidence of an ethnic gap in career progression.[197] The authors conclude that there is still an urgent need to tackle many types of racism, but particularly 'situated racism', which refers to prejudice and unequal treatment in local communities, and 'elite racism', which exists in the form of stereotyped assumptions and generalisations about different ethnic groups, which are reproduced by public figures and by the media and which have a major influence on public attitudes and behaviours, including those in the workplace. Everyday racism at a local level is evident in the sometimes humiliating treatment of Black and minority ethnic welfare users by public sector staff,[198] while discrimination and inequality are a daily reality for many refugees and asylum seekers in Britain.

The government has begun to take action to address the unequal life chances of ethnic minority communities. It is committed to developing an overarching community cohesion and race equality strategy,[199] and has adopted cross-cutting diversity policies in a range of areas, from employment to education to housing. For example, an influential report from the Strategy Unit in 2003 highlighted the durable unemployment among minority communities, and suggested a range of practical measures to address barriers faced by ethnic minority groups in the labour market.[200] The government's proposals for tackling discrimination and prejudice are summarised below. As with other aspects of its equalities agenda, New Labour deserves credit for the scale of its commitment to promoting racial equality, and has even begun to make progress in some areas, but the task of creating a genuinely inclusive society is one that is necessarily ongoing, and will require a long-term project of reform.

It is also important to be aware that the government's equalities agenda largely excludes asylum-seeking children and families. As Pamela Fitzpatrick warns, 'government asylum policy directly conflicts with policies on child welfare, social inclusion and anti-discrimination'.[201]

Although the government's anti-poverty strategy has succeeded in alleviating hardship for some marginalised groups, asylum seekers are more vulnerable to low income than other groups, as well as being at higher risk of suffering from poor health and of being forced to live in substandard accommodation.[202] Furthermore, since the right to work was withdrawn in 2002, those who are waiting for a decision on their asylum claim are denied the opportunity to improve their standard of living, and so are at even greater risk of being in poverty.[203] The rights of asylum seeker children and families are therefore in urgent need of protection.

Disability and poverty

Childhood disability can be both a cause and consequence of child and family poverty. Growing up in relative poverty is associated with an increased risk of impairment, and the additional costs of child disability are not adequately compensated for by welfare benefits targeted at child disability.[204]

One in 5 adults and one in 20 children in Britain are disabled in some way. Children with a disability include those with an 'intellectual disability', or a health problem which reduces their school attendance and increases their need for care.

- 73.3 per cent of families with disabled children have an income below the UK mean income, and 30.7 per cent suffered 'absolute low income' as defined by the government.[205]

- Families supporting children with a disability are 1.45 times more likely to live in poverty than other families. In 2001, families of children with a disability were more than twice as likely not to be home owners or have investments worth more than £20,000, and to be in debt or behind on bills payments.[206]

- Perhaps surprisingly, there is evidence to suggest that as many as 35 per cent of non-working lone parents have disabled children.[207]

Families with disabled children are more susceptible to poverty because of the difficulties of combining caring responsibilities with employment, and because of the additional costs associated with disability, such as the costs of 'paying for special foods, additional clothes, heating and laundry, special toys and equipment, transport, hospital visits and appointments, addressing safety issues, and paying for childcare and leisure activities.[208] As well as material deprivation, disabled children and their families are at a higher risk of suffering from social exclusion, as lack of resources can limit access to activities outside of the home, and may cause children to be housebound.[209] Families with disabled children are therefore more exposed to the problems associated with poverty and financial insecurity than other families, and may require additional forms of support to help them care for their children and meet the costs of disability.

- Living in a household with a disabled adult increases the average risk of child poverty from 19 per cent to 30 per cent (see section 2.6.2).

- 49 per cent of disabled people of working age are employed, compared to 81 per cent of non-disabled people.

- In 2003, 24 per cent of disabled people aged 16-24 had no qualifications at all, compared to 13 per cent of their non-disabled peers.

Children are also more exposed to poverty if they live with a disabled adult. Some disabled adults face barriers to employment due to lower than average educational qualifications, while in many cases having a disability affects their ability to gain work, either because of impairment or because of negative attitudes from employers. As well as affecting one's chances of earning income from employment, having a disability also increases the risk of material deprivation, as the higher costs associated with many forms of disability (including transport costs, special equipment and diets) mean that the same amount of income allows disabled people to consume fewer goods and services than non-disabled people.[210]

Proposals for reform to the benefit system for disabled children and adults include efforts to encourage greater take-up of benefits and a simplified system of benefit application.[211] Criticism of inadequate benefit levels have also promoted calls for an increased rate of Disability Living Allowance, to reflect the true costs of disability, and for increases in the allowances for carers, though as Northway observes, confusion at present over what counts as family income may create difficulties in assessing the adequacy of benefits.[212] Parents of disabled children may also need more targeted support to help them enter employment, for example, with meeting the costs of suitable childcare.

The government has recognised many of these issues and challenges in principle, and has set out proposals for seeking to transform the life chances of disabled people, based on four key areas: independent living; early years and family support; the transition to adulthood; and employment.[213]

Its strategy is underpinned by a pledge that, by 2025, disabled people should have full opportunities and choices to improve their quality of life and be respected and included as equal members of society.[214] A new Office for Disability Issues will also be established to coordinate government work on disability. While these proposals are to be welcomed, it is as yet too early to assess how far the reforms will go in adequately meeting the needs of disabled children and their families.

Place and poverty

Regional variations in the risk of poverty highlight the strong connections between poverty and place. Poverty rates are highest in parts of Inner London, while poverty is also more prevalent in the West Midlands and in northern regions, particularly the North East.[215]

Furthermore, the spatial concentration of some ethnic minority groups in certain deprived areas, or 'pockets' of poverty, illustrates the overlap between different categories of disadvantage. Over two thirds of England's Black and minority ethnic population live in the 88 most deprived local authority districts.[216] People living in deprived areas often have poor outcomes for health, education, employment, crime and housing. For members of ethnic minority communities living in deprived areas, the outcomes are often even worse. The reasons for these outcomes may reflect more than the sum of individual poverty: burdens and difficulties created by the daily reality of poverty may be exacerbated and compounded by a low quality physical environment.

There is disagreement, however, about the extent to which 'neighbourhood effects' operate independently of family and household factors. It may be the case, for example, that where people live 'reflects unobservable parental traits and attitudes that together influence later outcomes'.[217] Nevertheless, there are reasons to believe that location does exert an independent effect, and that where people live, including the 'lived experience' of poverty 'within the physical and social space of the neighbourhood',[218] does impact upon their life chances in various ways.[219] As discussed in previous chapters, living in a deprived area increases the likelihood of experiencing a range of problems, from substandard accommodation to poor quality services and facilities and high crime rates, each of which has consequences for other dimensions of life. With regard to health, for instance, the combination of lower quality health care services in the local area, physical ailments caused by substandard accommodation and stress caused by higher levels of crime, and fear of crime, may all contribute to worse health outcomes for residents. With regard to education, children from deprived areas are more likely to attend schools with 'disproportionate numbers of other low-income children, which may reduce school capacity to provide quality instruction, and expose students to negative peer effects that lower their educational performance'.[220] In addition, where people live may also affect their employment prospects, by limiting their social networks and because of physical barriers caused by poor transport links.

Government action to combat poverty of place has taken the form of area-based policies, such as the New Deal for Communities, to combat multiple deprivation in the most deprived neighbourhoods in the country. In 2001, the government committed itself to narrowing the gap between the poorest areas and the national average through its National Strategy for Neighbourhood Renewal, so that 'in 10 to 20 years no one is seriously disadvantaged by where they live'.[221] It has also recognised the need to integrate the diversity agenda into its neighbourhood renewal strategy, and is committed to engaging with different communities of interest, to involve Black and minority ethnic groups in the process of renewal.[222] Early findings suggest that progress is being made towards these goals,[223] though difficulties remain, particularly in relation to the recruitment and retention of skilled staff. [224]

Combating discrimination

As set out above, prejudice and discrimination not only exacerbate the experience of poverty for those on very low income, but also constitute a significant inequality in their own right, which affects people at all levels of income. Combating discrimination and prejudice against marginalised groups in society is therefore an urgent political priority, and one on which the government has started to take action. Much more needs to be done, however, to address the problem of discrimination against people in poverty.

Public attitudes and behaviour towards marginalised groups have shifted over the last thirty years, since the first Equality Commissions (the Commission for Racial Equality and Equal Opportunities Commission) were established. But continued evidence of the poor outcomes and discrimination faced by women, ethnic minority groups and disabled people – as well as discrimination on the grounds of religion and sexuality – reminds us that there is no room for complacency. Non-governmental organisations and bodies have an essential role to play in tackling prejudice by challenging cultural attitudes and assumptions, and preventing unfair treatment of people because of gender, disability or ethnicity. In addition, while the media may have an adverse effect insofar as it perpetuates and reproduces negative assumptions, it also has a potentially powerful positive role to play in challenging and breaking down those stereotypes.

But while a national strategy for combating discrimination and promoting equality requires the participation of multiple actors, the role of government in tackling institutional discrimination remains crucial. The government's commitment to eliminating discrimination and promoting equality is embodied in its plans to establish a single equality and human rights body, the Commission for Equality and Human Rights (CEHR), which will provide a single framework to tackle prejudice and promote good relations throughout British society.[225] The proposals for the CEHR have in the main been positively received – though with some notable exceptions – and most commentators accept in principle that there are good reasons to introduce a single framework to coordinate action on equality.[226] A single framework will particularly help those people who fall into more than one 'minority' category, such as disabled people from ethnic minorities, as studies have found that there are relatively few services which properly address the needs of these groups.[227]

The government has appointed a Discrimination Law Review (DLR) to consider the fundamental principles of discrimination legislation and its underlying concepts and to address long-held concerns about inconsistencies in the current anti-discrimination legislative framework. It will work to develop a simpler, fairer legal framework for tackling discrimination. The independent Equalities Review, chaired by Trevor Philips, is linked to this work and will investigate the long-term and underlying causes of disadvantage and inequality. It will report to the Prime Minister in summer 2006, making practical recommendations for change and providing essential background and research for the DLR, as well as informing the development of the CEHR.

These developments in tackling many forms of discrimination are to be welcomed. It is worth highlighting, however, that the impact of the government's equalities agenda may be contradicted at times by its action in other areas of policy, notably in the tone and language of government statements about immigration and asylum. As a report by the Council of Europe in 2000 highlighted, increasingly restrictive asylum and immigration laws may have contributed to an increase in racism in the UK, helping to create a general negative climate concerning asylum seekers and refugees.[228]

Finally, it is important to recognise the need to start looking at discrimination on the grounds of income poverty in the same way as gender or race or disability. Research evidence and the testimonies of people in poverty suggests that they still have the experience of being talked down to by professional 'experts', rather than being treated with respect and consideration. There is a need to challenge bureaucratic procedures that may discourage people on low incomes from becoming active and productive agents in their own right. In particular, the design and orientation of services and institutions around a needs-based approach, which assesses people on their *deficiencies* rather than their *capabilities* or *assets*, needs to be addressed, with greater emphasis given to participation by service-users (as opposed to merely cosmetic consultation exercises) in the design of services.

At an institutional level, there is a continued, urgent need for specific training to promote awareness amongst employees (including public sector workers, such as health workers, teachers, benefit officers, social workers etc.) of the humiliating and stigmatising effects of insensitive treatment.[229] A recent report by the Social Exclusion Unit explicitly acknowledges that everyone using public services has 'the right to be treated with respect' and puts forward proposals for ensuring successful interactions between disadvantaged adults and frontline staff.[230] But there is still a long way to go before mainstream public services operate across the board with the right levels of sensitivity, user involvement and innovation in this respect.

Amongst the general public, there is still much more that could be done to promote recognition of the discrimination experienced by people *in poverty* (as well as on other grounds), and to combat discriminatory attitudes of the public themselves towards people in poverty. Although the government has begun to take a lead on challenging other forms of discriminatory attitudes and practice, it has yet to take a similar lead on changing public attitudes towards people in poverty. Our deliberative research demonstrates that achieving this kind of shift in public attitudes is a very difficult but pressing task. There is a need for change, therefore, not just to policies and practice, but to the dominant ideas and beliefs in society.[231]

Notes

1   Ermisch *et al.* 2001; Plewis *et al.* 2001; Walker 2003.

2   Lareau 1997.

3   Some of the methodologies that are used are studies which compare the outcomes of twins, or of adopted and natural children,

to account for genetic effects. Alternatively, instrumental variable methods use 'natural' experiments or policy reforms to control for endogenous effects (see Blow *et al.* 2005) for a review of these different methods).

4 Investigating the relationship between higher education and later outcomes in employment and earnings, for example, it would not be possible to disentangle the effects of not completing a course at university on one's subsequent earnings in the labour market from unobservable differences in motivation or ability, because most factors that affect not completing a degree course (like low motivation or ability) invariably also affect wages in any event.

5 Wilkinson 2005, p. 84.

6 Low birth weight is defined by the World Health Organisation as a birth weight less than 2,500 grams, since below this value birth weight-specific infant mortality begins to rise rapidly (HDA 2003, p. 1). It is caused by either a short gestation period or retarded intrauterine growth (or a combination of both).

7 The Millennium Cohort Study is a new national longitudinal birth cohort study that is tracking the development of almost 19,000 babies born between September 2000 and January 2002.

8 Dex and Joshi 2005.

9 Mayhew and Bradshaw 2005.

10 North 2005.

11 Jefferis *et al.* 2002.

12 Stevens-Simon and Orleans 1999, cited in HDA 2003, p. 1.

13 HM Treasury 2002.

14 In particular, the relative importance of pre-conception and post-conception experience in utero is not yet fully understood and preconception may be important for policy too.

15 Acheson 1998.

16 Kramer 1987, cited in HDA 2003, p. 2.

17 Ravelli *et al* 1998 and Clarke *et al* 1998, cited in North 2005.

18 Dallison and Lobstein 1995.

19 Babies born to women who smoke weigh on average 200g less than babies born to non-smokers. Messcar 2001, cited in HDA 2003, p. 2.

20   Department of Health 1998.

21   Dex and Joshi 2005.

22   *Ibid.*

23   Infant Feeding 2000.

24   Marmot 2004.

25   Graham 1993.

26   Brynin 1999.

27   The health problems associated with substandard accommodation are discussed further in section 2.4.3.

28   Maantay 2003.

29   Weinstock 2001.

30   O'Connor *et al.* 2002.

31   The psychosocial risk factors identified here are explored further below.

32   Institute of Fiscal Studies 2005.

33   North 2005.

34   *Ibid.*

35   Department of Health 2004.

36   Department of Health 2002.

37   Department of Health 2004.

38   The Sure Start Maternity Grant is available to pregnant women or their partners if they are on income support, income-based Job Seekers Allowance, Pension Credit, Child Tax Credit at a rate higher than the family element or Working Tax Credit where a disability or severe disability element is included in the award.

39   Health Development Agency 2003.

40   Feinstein 2003.

41   Unicef UK Baby Friendly Initiative 2004.

42   HDA 2003.

43   North 2005.

44   Hamlyn *et al.* 2002.

45   Bradshaw and Mayhew 2005.

46   Hamlyn *et al.* 2002.

47 Hart and Risley 1995, p. 193, cited in Barry 2005.

48 *Ibid.*

49 Esping Anderson 2003, cited in Harker and Kendall 2003, p. 3.

50 As part of its research into the effects of pre-school education, the EPPE project developed an index to measure the quality of the home learning environment (HLE), which takes into account the range and type of activities in which parents and children are engaged (Sylva *et al.* 2004, p. 5).

51 In the EPPE project's research, the 'home learning environment' was only moderately associated with parents' educational or occupational level and was more strongly associated with children's intellectual and social development than either parental education or occupation.

52 Sylva *et al.* 2004, p. 1.

53 As the authors note, this finding underpins the work in programmes such as Local Sure Start and Children's Centres that target areas of high social disadvantage (Sylva *et al.* 2004, p. 5). Provision of care and education in the early years is discussed in section 3.2.2 below.

54 Ghate and Hazel 2002.

55 Waldfogel 2004, p.5.

56 A different problem is that other parents who would like to return to work cannot do so because they cannot find good quality affordable childcare that meets their needs. Prentice 2004, p. 34.

57 Moss 2001; Moss 2005.

58 Equal Opportunities Commission 2005.

59 Shelter 2005.

60 Bornstein 1995; Bradley 1995, cited in Duncan and Brooks-Gunn 2000, p. 190.

61 Women's Budget Group 2005; Ghate and Hazel 2002.

62 Wadsworth 1991, cited in Wilkinson 2005, p. 186.

63 Formal centre-based provision is varied, and includes: play groups; 'integrated' centres which fully combine education and care; local authority day nurseries; private day nurseries; or nursery schools and nursery classes; while school aged children may be placed in

out-of-school clubs. Of course, the actual range of options available to parents will depend on the local area – not all these varieties will be available in all places.

64 Research investigating mothers' use of childcare reflects the commonly held assumption that childcare within couples is the mother's responsibility. But there are good reasons to challenge this assumption: for example, as we explore in section 2.6.8, a gendered division of childcare responsibilities, increases women's vulnerability to poverty.

65 Brewer and Shaw (IFS)

66 Waldfogel 2004,.

67 Sylva *et al.* 2004.

68 Howes 1988; Hofferth and Phillips 1991; NICHD Early Child Care Research Network 1997, 1998; Ramey & Ramey 1998, cited in Duncan and Brooks-Gunn 2000, p. 190

69 Brooks-Gunn *et al.* 1994; Burchinal *et al.* 1997; Lazar & Darlington 1982; Ramey & Ramey 1998, cited in Duncan and Brooks-Gunn 2000, p. 190.

70 Benasich *et al.* 1992, cited in Duncan and Brooks-Gunn 2000, p. 190.

71 The project takes into account the contribution to children's development of child and family background factors such as birth weight, gender, and parental qualifications and occupations (Sylva *et al.* 2004, p. 2).

72 Children made more progress in settings with better qualified staff, with a trained teacher as manager and a good proportion of trained teachers on the staff, and where there were warm, interactive relationships between staff and children (Sylva *et al.* 2004).

73 Sylva *et al.* 2004, p. 5.

74 Meyers *et al.* 2004, cited in Waldfogel 2004, p. 4.

75 Bel & Finch 2004.

76 Polly Toynbee, The *Guardian*, Wednesday 13 July 2005.

77 The government's Ten Year Strategy for early years and childcare, Choice for parents, the best start for children, contains proposals based on four key themes: choice and flexibility; availability; quality and affordability.

78 Quarmby 2003; Balls 2005.

79 National Audit Office 2004.

80 At present, the childcare element of the Working Tax Credit covers 70 per cent of eligible childcare costs up to a ceiling (increased for the second child but not beyond that), and is also subject to withdrawal as family income rises. From April 2006, the childcare element will be expanded to cover 80 per cent of costs. It is available where a lone parent or both parents in a couple do at least 16 hours' paid work each week, and is available until the September following the child's 15th birthday.

81 NESS 2004, p. 3.

82 *Guardian*, 13 September 2005

83 Anning *et al.* 2005.

84 Although educational inequalities are not exhaustive of the inequalities facing children of school-age (as indicated in Figure 7), our focus on educational inequalities in this section reflects the importance of educational outcomes and experiences for children's well-being and later life chances.

85 The focus on educational inequalities in this section reflects the importance of educational outcomes and experiences for children's later life chances. It is also worth acknowledging that educational inequalities are not exhaustive of the inequalities facing children of school-age, as indicated in Figure 7. But limitations of space and time have obliged us to focus primarily on these inequalities, because of the importance of educational outcomes and experiences for children's well-being and their later life chances.

86 Goldthorpe 2003.

87 Ridge 2002.

88 DfES 2003.

89 Warren and Gillborn 2005.

90 Pupils are entitled to free school meals if their parents receive: income support; income-based jobseeker's allowance; support under part VI of the Immigration and Asylum Act 1999; child tax credit, but are not entitled to working tax credit and have an annual income that does not exceed a set figure (as assessed by the Inland Revenue). Pupils are also entitled to free school meals if they

receive income support or income-based jobseeker's allowance in their own right.

91 Gillborn & Mirza 2000, p. 18.

92 Parent involvement in children's schooling can be measured for example by the amount of parent-child discussion, parent involvement in parent-teacher organisations, monitoring, and more direct parent involvement in school activities (such as speaking to a teacher or counsellor). Greater parent contact with the school system may suggest that parents are interested in their child's education, though it may also indicate poorer student performance. Hango 2005, p. 3.

93 According to McNeal (1999), the dyadic relationships between the parent and child, and between parents and teachers can be conceptualised as 'social capital', because extended social networks act as 'potential sanctioning agents for maintaining the norm of investment and caring for children'.

94 Annette Lareau (1997) reports the findings of an intensive, qualitative US study of home-school relationships in the first and second grades of a school in a working-class area and a school in an upper-middle-class area. Although all parents involved in the research, shared a desire to promote their children's educational success, parents in the two schools had different views about the level of education wished to see for their children. The study also found that parents in the middle-class school were much more likely to be closely involved in their children's schooling.

95 ATD Fourth World 2000.

96 Hango 2005, p. 14.

97 See http://www.feedmebetter.com.

98 BMA 2003, cited in Shelter 2005, p. 19.

99 ONS 1999.

100 Shelter 2005.

101 Shelter 2005.

102 Elder 1974; McLoyd 1990.

103 ONS 1999.

104 SEU 2004.

105 Ball & Vincent 2001; Van Zantan 2005.

106 Aggleton and Whitty 1985; Anyon 1981; Apple 1979; Erickson and Mohatt 1982 etc. cited in Lareau1997, p. 703.

107 Ridge 2002.

108 Mayo 2005.

109 Stoate and Jones 2002.

110 A recent Ofcom report, *Childhood Obesity – Food Advertising in Context*, acknowledges that there may be indirect effects of television advertising on children's health and diet, though it concludes that the direct effects on food consumption are modest.

111 Schor 2004; Mayo 2005.

112 Fabian Commission on Life Chances and Child Poverty 2005.

113 Ridge 2002.

114 OECD 2001.

115 Gorard 2003.

116 Education Guardian 18.10.2005.

117 NPI http://www.npi.org.uk/projects.htm.

118 The Sutton Trust 2005.

119 Mortimore, 2001, p. 3.

120 Sefton 2004.

121 Bingley *et al*. 2005.

122 Barnados *et al*. 2005.

123 *Ibid*, p. 3.

124 HMT 2004.

125 Higher levels of qualifications increase the chances of employment, and raise average earnings potential. In 2003, 80 per cent of working-age people in the UK with a degree were in employment compared with 50 per cent of those with no qualifications. In addition, those with a degree had average gross weekly earnings of £632 in full-time employment, compared with £298 for those without higher qualifications (ONS 2004c).

126 Jo Blanden, Paul Gregg and Stephen Machin (2005) explore changes in educational inequality over time by comparing the outcomes of three different cohorts (who were born in 1958, 1970 and late 1970s,

who turned 16 in 1974, 1984 and 1995/6 respectively). Their analysis shows that educational inequality at 16 – measured in terms of the gap in the staying on rate between those in the most and least affluent 20 per cent of the population – has declined for the more recent cohorts.

127 DfES 2005.

128 Connexions 2004.

129 Rennison *et al.* 2005.

130 Goldthorpe, Jackson, Erikson and Yaish 2004.

131 The assumption here is that the rational choice for young people to make at 16 would be to continue education, given the financial rates of return to gaining upper secondary qualifications and higher education degrees (cf. Heckman 2005).

132 The assessment of risk – costs, benefits and probabilities – is critical to decision-making. Goldthorpe (1996) argues that the consequences for a failed attempt at an academic qualification, including the additional costs and risk of exclusion from vocational alternatives, are more serious for those from working class backgrounds than those from middle classes.

133 Goldthorpe 1996, p. 493.

134 Careers services within and outside of schools and colleges are also an important source of information about the financial costs of higher education.

135 MORI 2005.

136 *Ibid.*, p. 9.

137 Rennison *et al.* 2005.

138 Dearden *et al.* 2005.

139 Connexions: 2004.

140 DfES 2005.

141 MORI 2005.

142 Demographic and poverty statistics in this section are drawn from DWP 2005.

143 Throughout this section, incomes are equivalised using the McClements scale to account for different households' size and

composition. For details see the HBAI methodology appendix, available at http://www.dwp.gov.uk/asd/hbai/hbai2004/appendicies.asp.

144 Wilkinson 2005.

145 Each bar represents the number of people living in households with equivalised weekly disposable income.

146 Income is equivalised to take into account different household sizes. These figures are the equivalent for a family of two adults with no children.

147 Brewer, Goodman *et al.* 2004.

148 Mulgan 2000.

149 The New Deals, launched in 1998, were originally focused on young people and the longer-term unemployed, but have subsequently been extended to other groups with relatively low employment rates including lone parents, disabled people, partners of benefit claimants and those over 50 years old. The New Deals are structured around personal advisers, who support job seekers with the process of searching for work, and if this is unsuccessful with addressing their barriers to employment such as lack of training and experience. Some New Deal programmes involve an element of compulsion, where failure to participate after a specified period of receiving unemployment benefits leads to sanctions. Jobcentre Plus, launched in 2002, is designed to integrate the activities of claiming benefits with searching for work and contributes to the goal of 'making work pay' through such measures as personal advisers to all benefit claimants of working age. Reforms to Jobseeker's Allowance, a key out-of-work benefit, have increased the degree of compulsion on unemployed people to actively search for work even before they enter a New Deal programme, and the government has indicated that it wishes to develop this approach further (HMT 2005, p.91).

150 Dorsett 2003; Wilkinson 2003, Dorsett 2004.

151 Corkett *et al.* 2005.

152 Jones 2005.

153 This is not to suggest that the function of benefits is solely vertical redistribution, however important this may be. Some benefits have

other functions, such as horizontal equity, which are also important to keep in mind.

154 Crawford & Shaw 2004.

155 Adam and Brewer 2004.

156 The Child Tax Credit is annualised and is therefore not usually described as a weekly amount. However, it examples are given here as weekly amounts for the purposes of comparison.

157 Note that this figure does not include the additional element for the child under one year old. Note also that the government's intention is for Child Tax Credit ultimately to replace child additions in means-tested benefits for those out of work.

158 Jones 2005, table eight.

159 Wealth is the term used for the ownership of assets. Assets may be held in the form of financial assets, such as savings and investments in shares (which may yield a flow of current income), or pension rights (which provide an entitlement to a future income flow), or in the form of non-financial assets, of which housing ownership is the principal kind. Housing wealth provides a significant source of inherited wealth, income in kind and cash income when properties are sold. Marketable assets exclude pensions, as these cannot be drawn on before retirement.

160 Post tax income figures from ONS, marketable wealth figures from HM Revenue and Customs series C estimates.

161 See section 3.5 for details.

162 Atkinson (2003, p. 1) charts the share of the top income groups over the course of the twentieth century, and shows how major equalisation of the first three-quarters of the century in the UK was reversed in the last quarter, 'taking the shares of the top income groups back to levels of inequality found fifty years ago'.

163 Women's Budget Group 2005, p. iii.

164 Lister 2005.

165 Women's Budget Group, 2005, Women's and children's poverty: making the links, Women's Budget Group.

166 Graham 1993.

167 Ridge 2002.

168 DWP 2004.

169 Bradshaw *et al*. 2003.

170 Women's Budget Group, 2005.

171 Purcell 2005.

172 ONS 2005. The gender pay gap is defined as the percentage difference in hourly earnings between the average (mean) women's and men's earnings.

173 ONS 2004.

174 Equal Opportunities Commission 2003.

175 Bennett 2005.

176 Lissenburgh 2003. The study also highlights a particularly high pay gap between males and females working part-time: whereas women in full-time jobs would see their pay increase by almost 10 per cent if their human capital attributes were rewarded in the same way as men's, the comparative figure for female part-timers is just over 15 per cent.

177 Bennett 2005, p. v.

178 DWP/Women and Work Commission 2005, p. 18.

179 The Women and Work Commission was originally due to publish its final report and recommendations in September 2005, but these will now be published early in 2006.

180 DWP 2005.

181 Commission for Racial Equality 2005.

182 Paxton & Dixon 2004.

183 DWP 2005.

184 Youth Cohort Study, Department for Education and Skills. 2003.

185 *Ibid*.

186 Annual Local Area Labour Force Survey, ONS 2004.

187 Department for Education and Skills.

188 Cabinet Office 2003.

189 Cabinet Office 2003.

190 Warren and Gillborn 2005.

191 Aymer & Okitikpi 2001.

192 Gillborn and Youdell 2001.

193 Gillborn 1990.

194 Youdell 2001.

195 Pilkington 1999, p. 417.

196 Equal Opportunities Commission 2003.

197 Bhavnani, Mirza, & Meetoo, 2005.

198 Lister 2004, p. 63.

199 CRE 2004.

200 Cabinet Office 2003.

201 Fitzpatrick 2005, p. 92.

202 Hills and Stewart 2005.

203 Until 2002, asylum seekers were entitled to work if they had been waiting for more than six months for a decision on their asylum claim.

204 Dobson and Middleton 1998.

205 Woolley 2004.

206 Emerson and Hatton 2002.

207 Prime Minister's Strategy Unit 2005.

208 Northway 2005, p. 83.

209 Northway 2005, p. 84.

210 Lister 2004, p. 65.

211 Preston 2005.

212 Northway 2005.

213 Prime Minister's Strategy Unit 2005.

214 *Ibid*.

215 DWP 2005.

216 ODPM 2005.

217 Berube 2005, pp. 4-5.

218 Lister 2004, p. 69.

219 Berube 2005.

220 Berube 2005, p. 5. See Lupton (2004) for analysis of the links between poverty, place and poor educational attainment.

221 Cabinet Office 2001.

222 ODPM 2004.

223 NCD National Evaluation Team 2004.

224 *Ibid*, p. ii.

225 The new Commission will replace and incorporate the work of the three existing equality bodies – the Commission for Racial Equality, the Disability Rights Commission and the Equal Opportunities Commission. The government intends for the CEHR to be established in 2007, for all areas except those for which the Commission for Racial Equality (CRE) is responsible. These areas will remain with the CRE until April 2009, when the CRE's responsibilities will transfer to the CEHR.

226 Strong reservations to the original proposals were expressed by the Commission for Racial Equality – and echoed by the Refugee Council – during the Fairness For All consultation period. While the government's revised proposals have addressed some of these concerns, the CRE has continued to press for a higher priority for race equality, calling for a similar committee for race to be established alongside the proposed Disability Committee, and has expressed concerns about a number of other issues (see CRE2006; Refugee Council 2004).

227 Research by the Joseph Rowntree Foundation has developed a body of work looking at race equality within the context of disability, which has highlighted the lack of existing services and the fact that many agencies have tended to operate within the confines of their original remit of race or disability (see, for example, Roberts and Harris; Bignall *et al.*; Hussain *et al.* ; Bignall and Butt; Chamba *et al*).

228 CRI 2001, cited in Fitzpatrick 2005, p. 105.

229 One positive example of this is a project involving families in poverty in social work education, which has been jointly organised by a number of anti-poverty groups and a university department. See ATD Fourth World *et al.* 2005.

230 Social Exclusion Unit 2005.

231 ATD Fourth World *et al.* 2005.

Part Three:
Closing the gap in life chances

Introduction

Narrowing inequalities in life chances will depend upon a coherent and focused series of policy interventions across the life course, underpinned by a sustained and increased political commitment to make the UK more equal. Focusing public services on closing the gap in life chances will be an important part of this. Improving the income of parents will also be vital, and this will mean increasing direct financial support for families, especially those on low incomes, as well as helping parents into paid employment.

As explained above, the causes of child poverty and unequal life chances result from a set of overlapping problems such as poor parental educational and health status, a deleterious neighbourhood environment, barriers to employment, low pay and inadequate and poorly taken up benefits as well as wider inequalities in rewards and status. While these causes are complex and interlocking, there is a wide range of policy tools which can have an impact on these inequalities and help to achieve more equal life chances for children from different backgrounds. Too often, however, public policy is simply not focused on addressing these issues, and in some cases it actively worsens the situation.

To be effective, interventions in different policy areas must add up to more than the sum of their parts to form a coherent and effective strategy to tackle inequalities in life chances across the life course. As we argue here, the early years agenda and the recent unprecedented focus on it are important; but policies for the early years are not enough.

On the one hand, the early years are already too late to start addressing problems which begin before conception. We need to address the factors which affect children's life chances before they are born. This will take government into as yet uncharted territory, seeking to improve the lives of *parents-to-be, especially young and pregnant women*, whose own health, financial security and well-being are central to the life chances of the next generation.

On the other hand, reforms in early childcare and pre-school education must be pursued in conjunction with other policies if momentum is to be maintained from early years into primary and secondary schooling and beyond. At present, schools policy, for example, is not sufficiently focused on closing the stark gaps in attainment for children from low-income and low socio-economic status backgrounds or on achieving an inclusive educational experience for all children.

The ability of government to pursue a coherent policy agenda depends in turn on building and sustaining sufficient support and legitimacy for a national mission to end poverty and tackle life chance inequalities. The government's 2020 target to eradicate child poverty, and its interim target of halving it by 2010, are very challenging. Our research into public attitudes shows that the public has complex attitudes to poverty, including initial scepticism about the extent and importance of income poverty in the UK; negative stereotypes of 'the poor'; and limited belief in the effectiveness of government action to combat poverty. It will be a critical political challenge to build the broad and durable public consensus that will be necessary to sustain the project to eradicate child poverty over the next 15 years.

Focusing the government's anti-poverty strategy on tackling child poverty has enabled important progress to be made. The public tends to have greater sympathy for poor children than for their parents, who remain subject to strong stereotypes and myths about the 'undeserving poor'.

But family poverty is a more accurate description of the problem we are trying to eradicate. Ending child poverty depends centrally on what happens to families and parents. Moreover, there is no magical social policy device that can tackle the cycle of deprivation for families and parents-to-be whilst leaving everyone else out. Ultimately, politicians and policy-makers need to acknowledge that progress towards ending poverty and creating equal life chances for children depends on creating a fairer and more equal society for us all.

In this final part of the report, we make fourteen recommendations for public policy, of which Recommendation 1 and Recommendation 2 relate to the task of eradicating child poverty and improving life chances more broadly; Recommendation 3 to Recommendation 7 correspond to different stages of the life course (as set out in Part Two), beginning with the period before birth; and Recommendation 8 to Recommendation 14 set out proposals for improving financial support to children and adults, and narrowing inequalities in income and wealth more broadly. The recommendations are of different types: in certain policy areas we urge the government to adopt new objectives, while in other areas we set out more substantive proposals for reform.

A new life chances strategy for equality

We have argued that addressing poverty is vital to improving children's life chances, and that improving outcomes for children will in turn play a central role in breaking the cycle through which disadvantage leads to poverty. We therefore wholeheartedly support the government's commitment to end child poverty by 2020, and recognise the major achievements already made in reducing the number of children living in poverty.

The 2007 Comprehensive Spending Review will make important choices about government spending and priorities for this parliamentary term. The government has announced that the review will be informed by a strategic review of the major challenges facing the UK, leading to a report on these challenges to be published in 2006. The Treasury has already identified some of the major issues which this review will address: a rapid increase in the old age dependency ratio; increasing cross-border trade and competition; the increasing pace of technological change; terrorism and global conflict; and increasing pressures on our natural resources and global climate.

Poverty and unequal life chances need to be identified as central to the review and their eradication as national priorities for the UK. One of the key arguments made by this Commission has been that poverty and inequality issues have not featured sufficiently prominently in public debate. Indeed, in our view this may now represent the most significant barrier to the government's ability to achieve its ambitious objectives on poverty and inequality. The build-up to a Comprehensive Spending Review which will need to make the case for increased resources to tackle poverty is a vital moment to increase the public and political salience of these issues and to build support for tackling and reducing poverty and inequalities.

In addition to reaffirming its commitment to the goal of eradicating child poverty by 2020, and halving it by 2010, the government will also need to update and refresh the Child Poverty Review of 2004. Our analysis of the policy and political challenges strongly suggests that the scope of the review should be broadened at this time. Unequal life chances have not been considered in a cross-departmental way and should thus be specifically addressed as part of this work. In the absence of any requirement to report on these issues, there is little accountability for politicians who can safely assert their belief in the project of equal life chances for all children.

It would therefore be a major step forward for the government to publish an annual review that reports on progress across government towards improving and equalising life chances, with a broader inequalities focus and remit than previous official cross-cutting reviews of poverty. An annual review of life chances could form part of the existing 'Opportunity for All' series, which details progress on the government's strategy to tackle poverty and social exclusion, or it could stand on its own – a new 'Life chances for All'.

▶ **Recommendation 1**

The government's child poverty commitments must be identified as a central national priority in framing the 2007 Comprehensive Spending Review, reaffirming the commitment to halving child poverty by 2010 relative to its 1999 baseline and eradicating child poverty by 2020. The government should, during 2006, conduct a cross-cutting and cross-departmental **Review of Life Chances in the UK**, *and of the government activity necessary to narrow gaps in life chances.*

▶ **Recommendation 2**

The government should institute a regular **annual Life Chances Audit** *which details progress on improving and equalising life chances for children and young people in the UK. It would bring together evidence on all the main strands of work across govern-*

ment that address inequalities in life chances, and would inform media and public debate about the key facts and trends in inequalities in Britain.

The public spending review is also an important moment for the government to review the Public Service Agreements targets regime. This is one of the key mechanisms for government to prioritise and co-ordinate its activity, and to seek to give strategic coherence to its overall policy approach. From a life chances perspective, a key issue is the outcomes experienced by different social groups in public services and their impact on life chances. If our concern is with inequalities in life chances, this needs to be recognised in government measures and targets. Public service targets can take a number of different approaches. Some **general targets** (such as to increase the proportion of students who gain 5 GCSEs at A*-C to 60 per cent by 2008) may not refer to the disadvantaged specifically at all; **floor targets** (such as that 30 per cent of the 16 year olds in *every* school achieve five GCSEs at grades A* to C by 2008) seek to raise standards at the bottom, while **inequality targets** try to narrow the gap between more and less disadvantaged people or areas.

It is obvious that general targets are consistent with increasing inequality: for example an increasing proportion of children can achieve good outcomes whilst the gap between them and those who fail can get wider. But it is also important to recognise that floor targets do not necessarily reduce inequalities either: for example every school could achieve the floor target whilst the gap between the best and worst continues to widen because the best improve faster. So the existing suite of floor targets across government departments represents an important set of measures to improve the position of those who are currently disadvantaged, but they do not address inequality per se. In a sense, they are the life chances counterpart to the absolute low income target, and are necessary but not sufficient.

In some important areas, the government has already adopted explicit commitments to close gaps and reduce inequalities in life chances. The Department of Health has a number of ambitious Public Service Agreements targeted on health inequalities, which have proved particularly challenging to meet. These include targets to narrow the gap in heart disease and cancer mortality rates between the fifth of local areas with the worst outcomes and the average, and targets to narrow the gaps in infant mortality and life expectancy at birth between people in routine and manual occupations and the population as a whole. The Department for Work and Pensions meanwhile has a number of PSA targets to reduce the difference between the overall employment rate and the rate for disadvantaged groups including lone parents, ethnic minorities, older people, those with low qualifications and those living in disadvantaged areas as well as disabled people.

An effective inequalities strategy should extend this approach across government. A crucial policy area where there is currently the least focus on inequality, at least at the level of PSA targets, is that of education. The Department for Education & Skills does have two inequality focused targets: first, it aims to narrow the gap between children's development at Foundation Stage (approximately age five) between the fifth of most deprived local authority areas and the rest of England; and second, it is committed to narrowing the gap in a number of later educational outcomes between looked after children and their peers. But there are no inequality targets for the vast majority of school age children. Inequality targets in this area should not be rejected on the basis that they will lead to 'levelling down' – in other key areas of policy this issue is already dealt with by setting objectives so that they can only be achieved by improving the situation of the disadvantaged, not worsening the position of those already achieving good outcomes.

Tackling inequalities in life chances across the life course

3.3.1 Before birth – preventing inequalities at the start of life

The government's Child Poverty Review sets out a good starting point for tackling child poverty and breaking the cycle of disadvantage, beginning with the first years of life, but it is not exhaustive of what is needed to achieve the government's own goal of eradicating child poverty. We argue that the next stage of the government's strategy against child poverty must begin to address inequalities in life chances more explicitly, and must look at the period *before* birth, given the importance of factors which affect children's life chances before they are born.

We have seen that class inequalities strongly affect life chances at birth – with striking class gradients in infant mortality rates and the birth-weight of babies. Maternal health and well-being, including the pre-pregnant weight of the mother (and indeed her own birth weight) are principal determinants of a baby's birth weight and its subsequent health. So a life chances strategy must begin by improving the health of women of child-bearing age, before they conceive, as well as focusing support where it can be most effective during pregnancy. In the long-term, increasing the birth weight of the *next* generation will have an impact on health across the life cycle, including potential benefits for *their* children. Just as inequalities at birth currently accumulate through generations, success in breaking the cycle of poverty and disadvantage would have a cumulative impact across generations to come.

The government has recognised that the health of mothers is the key to low birth weight rates, and that interventions to promote optimum nutrition and smoking cessation during pregnancy are key to reducing the risk of low birth weight. It has also recognised the importance of reducing teenage pregnancy rates, by setting national targets to reduce the teenage conception rate by 2010 and to increase the participation of teenage parents in education, training or work, to reduce their risk of long-term social exclusion.[1] Effectively addressing these problems depends in part on recognising the impact of low income and the additional stresses of low social status.

Maternity support during pregnancy will be too late to have an impact on the development of the foetus during the first trimester of pregnancy, and the health of women prior to conception is ultimately just as important as the quality of care during pregnancy. A key factor in maternal health is diet and nutrition. The causes of poor diet are complex – from low public understanding of what constitutes a healthy and balanced diet to lack of access to fresh, healthy food, due to structural factors such as the location of shops and (un)availability of good public transport. Education is clearly important – maternity support services can provide advice and information for mothers-to-be on healthy eating during pregnancy, and schools play an important long-term role much earlier. But however important it may be, education cannot be sufficient, since "knowing about a nutritious diet is useless if it cannot be paid for."[2] It is therefore absolutely vital that people have the financial means to eat healthily – which is not the case now. We will return to these issues in our later recommendations on income.

Smoking during pregnancy powerfully affects the life chances of the unborn child, and a strong relationship exists between smoking during pregnancy and socio-economic status.[3] The evidence of the adverse impact of smoking by parents-to-be, and parents, on life chances shows the importance of government continuing to seek to reduce smoking rates. There are tensions here for progressives, as tobacco taxes are highly regressive – but the health evidence shows why an anti-smoking strategy is important. One of the most important issues to be addressed is why anti-smoking strategies have to date proved less effective with working-class smokers than other social groups. More focus is also required on finding out which health promotion strategies prove effective in persuading young men and women to give up smoking, or not take it up in the first place. We then need to focus new resources on this key early determinant of later life chances for both children and future parents.

The UK currently aims for a very high number of antenatal visits by pregnant women to GPs and midwives – 13, compared to nine in many other EU countries. There is little evidence that this high average rate has achieved better outcomes in terms of overall infant mortality or other early health outcomes. But pregnant women on low incomes have greater difficulty in accessing maternity care and antenatal services, due to transport difficulties, long inflexible hours or caring duties. Antenatal support and resources could therefore be refocused to concentrate more on disadvantaged mothers who suffer the worst outcomes.

Current pre-natal services are strongly focused on health and less on the wider requirements of parents. Refocusing antenatal support services on parents at greater risk should allow this remit to be widened to address the frequently expressed desire among parents and parents-to-be for better general parenting support as opposed to medical supervision. This would, however, require nurses and health visitors to expand their role as the bridge to other support. Such focused early support could be used to increase the take up of high quality childcare at the next stage of the life course. Whilst challenging, this agenda would fit well with the trend towards the integration of children's services at local level.

► **Recommendation 3**

The current pattern of maternity support should be refocused so that it is more concentrated on disadvantaged mothers whose children suffer the worst outcomes, especially in terms of low birth weight and infant mortality. This additional support should be better linked to wider early years' services such as high quality childcare as well as parenting support programmes.

Sure Start projects can now extend help and support to pregnant women as well as parents with children. The introduction of this kind of targeted service for low-income pregnant women is to be welcomed, though needs to be extended to those women living outside areas of deprivation who are not currently eligible to receive this support.

3.3.2 Infancy and the early years

The importance of the role of parents, and their relationships with their children, for life chances can hardly be overestimated. Differences in parental resources, skills and the home environment play a crucial role in the unequal development of cognitive ability between children of higher-income and lower-income parents by the time they start school, even where the poorer children were brighter to start with. These disadvantages which arise in infancy and early childhood accumulate across the life course, to the long-term detriment of children's life chances. Narrowing the pre-school gap in cognitive, vocabulary and linguistic ability appears a daunting task. Indeed, some may doubt how policy interventions can compensate children or effectively replicate the wide range of advantages which their better-off peers receive. But as discussed in section 2.2, recent research by the EPPE study shows that it is possible to make progress in this direction – indeed, that this has already been achieved.

The government's early years strategies have begun to demonstrate that coherent policy interventions can make a difference, as has the focus on increasing the availability of high quality, affordable childcare. The extension of paid maternity leave to nine months by 2007, and the further goal of increasing this to twelve months by the end of the current Parliament, will help more mothers access the new rights to longer maternity leave. But more needs to be done to address economic pressures to return to work, particularly because the children who would benefit most from support will find that their parents are least able to take up opportunities for extended leave. There is also a need to reconsider leave arrangements for lone parents, for example by providing extra leave allowances for lone parents to make up for the lack of a second parent's leave.

In terms of the share of leave between parents, the government has made provision for up to six months 'additional paternity leave' (APL), the first three months of which may be paid at a flat rate, subject to certain conditions.[4] But to be eligible, the mother must go back to work after her six months maternity leave and entitlement to paid APL depends on her entitlement to statutory maternity pay/allowance. Entitlement therefore depends on the mother having been working prior to birth (otherwise she will not have maternity rights to share) and on being willing to share provision in this way. The Equal Opportunities Commission makes a convincing case for greater rights for new fathers, including shared parental leave rights in the second six months of a child's life, whether or not the mother was working before the birth.[5] Allowing shared parental leave rather than transferable *maternity* leave is important, as it signals that caring is the role of both parents. In our view, although the proposals in the new Work and Families Bill represent an improvement on previous arrangements, the option of partially transferable maternity leave is still second best to adequately paid parental leave that is transferable between the mother and father. In addition, given financial and other constraints, such as working practices and the culture in many organisations, it is not clear whether fathers will be sufficiently motivated to take up their new leave entitlements (which are in any case dependent on the mother's entitlement). We therefore believe that parental leave should include an element of 'use it or lose it' leave for fathers to encourage take-up. Addressing the current gender imbalance in parenting responsibilities in the early years is a priority, in our view, because under existing arrangements mothers who take up entitlements to extended leave risk damaging their future labour market position, to the long-term detriment of themselves and their families' income.

▶ Recommendation 4

*There should be a statutory right to a year's **paid parental leave** which is transferable between parents, including an element of 'use it or lose it' leave reserved for fathers. This would help low-income parents take up their leave entitlements and encourage fathers to accept greater parental responsibilities.*

The key source of objection to such a proposal is likely to be from business representatives facing disruption of their employment patterns. It might thus make sense to pilot the extension of paid parental leave in a small number of areas of the country to evaluate the real impacts on businesses and to learn how such impacts can be imaginatively minimized.

Furthermore, if the aim is to facilitate greater involvement of both parents, it is important to consider the level at which it is set. Under current proposals, the rate would be £106 a week, to be reimbursed to companies by the Treasury. But if we seriously want fathers to play a greater role in early parenting, paid leave will need to be set at levels close to that of existing wages. As this would be very expensive for those at the top end of the pay scale, a ceiling might be placed on levels of pay for the highest earners. Although horizontal equity would suggest a uniform policy for all, we believe that the priority should be on higher levels of income replacement for lower earners, as it is this group who currently face the most constrained choices and where it is most important to improve the quality of parent/child interactions.

Early childhood interventions have been a central focus of policy and academic interest in recent years, and there is a new consensus on the importance of high quality childcare in improving life chances. There have been large increases in the number of places in day nurseries, after-school provision and other forms of childcare. The present pattern of childcare provision has profound implications for children's life chances. Children who are already advantaged by greater resources in the home benefit more from formal childcare, while low income, lone parent and ethnic minority households are least likely to use formal childcare. Childcare tends to be weakest where it is most needed and where improvements in children's outcomes could be greatest.

Given how crucial this period is to prevent gaps in children's development opening up still further and to begin to reduce them, the strategy must be to move towards a system of universal childcare. This approach is also vital to promote maternal employment, which is a key means of improving families' incomes. In addition, universal high quality childcare should help to develop shared childhood experience as an important building block for future solidarity. The Scandinavian countries such as Sweden have long benefited from these interlocking benefits as a result of their long-term commitment to properly funded childcare delivered by highly qualified professionals.

In seeking to increase the affordability, availability and quality of childcare to parents, especially those on low incomes who currently face the greatest barriers, we believe that government policy relies too heavily at present on demand side investment. There have been considerable problems in matching accessible supply and demand, with parents reporting insufficient supply of childcare at the same time as childcare places (especially those with childminders) in some areas have closed due to insufficient take-up and demand, and because of problems with premises, recruiting and local factors.[6] More attention to sustainable supply of high quality places would imply a shift in funding away from subsidising parental demand through tax credits and towards the provision of direct grants to providers – either by increasing public provision or by subsidising other providers. Research from the US suggests that this would also have the result of lowering costs for parents and so increasing the affordability of childcare, and would have the additional gain of increasing the leverage over quality that the government is able to exercise.[7] There is, however, a need to review the quality of choice and availability of different types of provision, especially for parents with disabled children, who have particular needs and requirements, and minority ethnic groups who have traditionally made less use of formal, centre-based childcare than other groups.

▶ **Recommendation 5**

The UK should aspire to a system of universal high quality childcare, with government playing a role in both subsidising demand for childcare and in directly supporting the supply of places. However, public spending should be re-balanced from subsidising demand through tax credits, towards directly supporting the supply of high quality places. This would reduce costs for parents and provide a powerful mechanism for improving standards in the childcare sector.

3.3.3 Promoting better life chances for school-age children

For the vast majority of the child population, there are no inequality targets relating to children's education and development once they enter formal schooling. From the life chances perspective, this is a significant gap in public policy. While New Labour in power committed itself to tackling health inequalities early in its first term, a more sustained interest in narrowing the gap in attainment has been slower to emerge. One sign of a more sustained interest in tackling educational inequalities is the recognition given to the challenges identified by the Secretary of State in July 2005:

> "We must not and will not give up on all our efforts to raise average attainment to new record highs. ... But in addition, our aim – unequivocally – must be to ensure that the attainment gap at 11 begins to narrow."[8]

From a life chances perspective, what this signals is that the life chances framework can be usefully applied to schools policy. The overall objective would be similar to that set out by the Secretary of State: to continue to improve overall standards whilst improving the performance of the disadvantaged relative to that of their peers, thus closing the gap in attainment. But perhaps most striking is the disjuncture between this apparent appetite to tackle educational inequalities and the Department's formal objectives in terms of Public Service Agreements. If DfES is really 'the department for life chances', as proclaimed by the Secretary of State, then its objectives and targets should develop to reflect this. Changes in the headline targets would potentially have far-reaching implications, given that a key national mechanism for changing LEA and school behaviour is the audit, inspection and intervention system headed by Ofsted and the Audit Commission.

The next opportunity for changing Public Service Agreements will be the 2007 Comprehensive Spending Review. There is now a window of opportunity in which to develop targets to support the objective of improving the educational outcomes of disadvantaged children relative to their peers. Key questions include decisions about: what will be measured; when it will be measured; what disadvantaged groups will be targeted; what specific goals should be set; and what other policies will be necessary to support their achievement. It will be necessary to have a serious public debate over this period about educational inequality and the appropriate policy response. This would both maximise the chances of making the right policy decisions, and help to build public consent for what should be a very significant set of decisions.

Although we do not propose a specific set of targets in this report, our analysis points to a number of desirable characteristics. First, because educational inequalities are visible from an early age and persist throughout the school years, they should be measured and targeted from an early age onwards. This probably means developing a suite of targets from Foundation Stage through to Key Stage 4. Second, because it is possible to reduce inequalities at the area or school level without doing so at the individual level, targets should be set at the individual level if possible. For example, we should target the gap in outcomes between low income pupils and their peers, rather than (or as well as) between schools or areas with more and less deprived populations. Finally, measures of inequality should be principally focused on average individual attainment rather than floor targets (as it is, after all, possible to meet floor targets – such as the DfES target for 30 per cent of the 16 year olds in *every* school to achieve five GCSEs at grades A* to C by 2008 – while inequality increases between these schools and the rest). The government will rightly be concerned to reduce the overall number of low attaining pupils. But a key priority from a life chances perspective is to address not just low attainment but also the inequalities by which children from disadvantaged groups perform systematically worse than their peers. This means targeting the gaps.

▸ **Recommendation 6**

For the 2007 Comprehensive Spending Review, the government should develop Public Service Agreement targets to **reduce inequalities in educational attainment** *between disadvantaged groups and their peers from Foundation Stage onwards. These targets could be expressed in similar terms to those that already exist in relation to health outcomes and employment rates among disadvantaged groups.*

It is worth striking a cautionary note about relying too much on targets to drive up performance or to narrow gaps in achievement at school. There will always be a difficult balance to strike between having sufficient targets to support the necessary range of objectives, and limiting their number so that they are easily comprehensible both for the public and throughout the education system. The individual measures need to be carefully constructed so as to avoid providing perverse incentives, and particularly so that they are not prejudicial to pupils at the bottom of the achievement spectrum including those at risk of exclusion from school. Finally, the culture surrounding targets may be as important as the targets themselves. It would be of little use to introduce demanding inequality targets without an accompanying shift in political and public pressure to give them salience and legitimacy.

Targets in themselves would also have a limited effect in the absence of other policy measures to support them. On the one hand, policies can provide additional tools to enable LEAs and schools to improve the relative performance of disadvantaged pupils. Central to this will be the challenge of focusing resources on disadvantage, at the area, school and individual pupil level. On the other hand, they can provide incentives for actors such as LEAs, schools and teachers to achieve the objective. At present the schools inspection system, for example, is focused on average attainment and floor standards. LEAs and schools fear intervention as a result of failing the existing inspection regime. If we want to shift the focus of the education system, we will have to shift the focus of the audit and inspection regime.

Another key question for a progressive government is whether the principle of parental choice is in practice an effective way to narrow the gap in educational outcomes and promote more equal life chances. The choice agenda is central to the government's Education White Paper launched in October 2005, which contains proposals for structural reform of the schools system, to "create a system of independent non-fee paying state schools", and to allow popular schools to expand with the help of self-governing trusts run by businesses or groups of parents.[9] The aim of the proposals is to give parents more choice over which school their child attends, as well as to give schools more discretion over the admissions system. However, critics contend that a system based on greater local autonomy and parental choice is incompatible with progressive aims, given its tendency to favour parents with greater resources.

Certain aspects of the White Paper are to be welcomed, especially the priority that is given to the goal of "narrowing the gap in attainment at school level". Recognition is also given to "the role played by parental background in determining attainment and life chances", though the document tends to frame the debate more narrowly than we would wish, in terms of social mobility, which for reasons set out in Part One, we believe is problematic as an organising concept. The White Paper acknowledges that higher-income parents are often better able to "make the system work to their advantage", and makes specific proposals to assist children from lower-income families in accessing good schools through the extension of free school transport and the introduction of "dedicated choice advisors to help less well-off parents to exercise choice". However, we have serious doubts about the feasibility of the latter proposal, and wonder how receptive low-income parents would be to the idea of having 'means-tested' advisors to assist them.

In our view, the right objective for a progressive schools policy is to reduce the degree of social segregation in schools, both in terms of socio-economic status and in terms of prior ability. The proposals in the White Paper to make it easier "for schools to introduce banding into their admissions policies", might be viewed as a welcome step towards this goal, though as it is voluntary it remains to be seen whether schools opt to adopt it. More worryingly, there is no guarantee that the greater discretion given to schools over admissions will actually help the most disadvantaged children by achieving a better social and academic mix than exists at present, and may even exacerbate the problem. Finally, children for whom English is a second language especially need to be spread more evenly among schools, with greater financial incentives for schools to welcome them and to provide the extra teaching that ensures they make good progress.

We recognise that the goal of achieving a more balanced school intake will be challenging for a number of reasons. First, in many parts of the country housing is relatively socially segregated, which may lead to tension between this objective and the idea of 'neighbourhood schools'. This situation will take time to address, though over the long-term, housing policies are needed which can help achieve more balanced neighbourhoods.

Perhaps most importantly, we realise that the winners from the current system could be very resistant to changes which might reduce their current advantages, including the advantages that accrue from the private school system. Politically, it would be very difficult to reduce the chances of affluent parents successfully selecting the best schools, unless they were confident that this would not harm their own children's life chances. Improvements to schools and improvements to the social mix of schools will thus have to go hand in hand. Although this is an ambitious goal, it is not an issue which can be avoided. It is essential that social segregation by school does not undermine our attempts to improve the life chances of disadvantaged children.

We do not underestimate the political challenge of this problem. But if the government is committed to a choice agenda, it should explain how real choice can be extended to those who currently have little, and whom the current system actively disadvantages. A radical progressive choice policy could give precedence in the admissions system to low income parents, for example those entitled to income support, Job Seeker's Allowance or Working Tax Credit.

▶ **Recommendation 7**
Education policy should narrow inequalities in life chances and ensure it does not exacerbate them. **Admissions policies** *should be reviewed to reduce segregation by socio-economic background across the schools system.* **Education funding** *needs to more strongly follow need, and the* **schools audit and inspection** *system should develop a clearer focus on narrowing inequalities in educational outcomes between pupils from disadvantaged backgrounds and their peers.*

We also urge the government to do more to address inequalities in children's experience of school, as discussed in section 2.4. The extra costs of activities, equipment and clothing that parents are expected to meet for children at state schools can cause anxiety and embarrassment for parents and children alike.[10] Young people report feeling pressurised by intrusive advertising and marketing campaigns for 'branded' consumer goods.[11] There is a need therefore for greater awareness amongst teachers, as well as recognition amongst the wider public, of the stigmatising effects of poverty, and the ways in which lack of income can prevent children from fitting in at school and participating fully in school life.

3.3.4 Transforming the prospects of those whom education currently fails

In education, the key life chances priority is to transform the prospects of those whom education currently fails, and who leave or drop out of school without qualifications. We have seen that the incentives of the current system's focus on educational results may paradoxically exacerbate this, as schools and teachers focus on those around the threshold of five A*-C grade GCSEs.

Our concern for life chances across the life course means that we welcome the focus in the government's skills strategy for post-compulsory education on basic, lower and intermediate skills for those who miss out at school, with the central objective of raising the percentage of the adult population with level 2 qualifications (equivalent to five GCSEs at grade C or above), considered to be the level required for employability and access to life-long learning opportunities. But vocational qualifications reform is important if these vocational qualifications are to add to earnings power and increased opportunities to progress at work.

The proportion of young people who are 'NEET' – not in education, employment or training – has remained stubbornly constant since the mid 1990s despite significant increases in overall employment rates during this period. At the end of 2003 it is estimated that 9 per cent of 16-18 year olds were NEET, the same figure as for the end of 1994. This group of around 200,000 young people is the focus of considerable government attention, particularly through the Connexions service, but also through other agencies such as Sure Start Plus if they are young parents. Reducing the number of young people in this group will not only improve their own life chances, but could have knock-on effects for child poverty by helping to prevent the flow of children into poverty, thus making the 2020 target more feasible. It is also important, from a life chances perspective, to address the inequalities through which young people from lower socio-economic groups and other disadvantaged backgrounds are much more likely to become NEET than other young people.

Income inequalities and their impact on life chances

3.4.1 Benefits and tax credits

As set out in section 3.3.1, benefit rates for adults are important in part because of the links between the health of the parents (especially the mother) before the birth of the child and the child's own health and well-being. The causes of poor diet and ill-health during pregnancy are complex, and cannot be reduced to any single factor. But one policy measure that is essential to reduce poverty and thereby address the attendant health problems associated with very low income, is that of proper financial support for pregnant women.

▶ **Recommendation 8**
As a first step towards additional direct financial support, a 'pregnancy premium' to income support should be introduced for pregnant women. This would help address poverty among pregnant women and would promote the health of babies at the very start of life when they are most vulnerable.

In terms of financial support for children, there is a longstanding policy debate over the most appropriate way of directing additional resources. The significant extra resources made available since 1997 to support low income households have mostly come through the new tax credits, with Child Benefit being increased with inflation each year, except for a larger rise for the first child in 1999. For families with full entitlement, Child Tax Credit now makes up a far higher proportion of their income than Child Benefit.

In our view, the government's current commitment to increasing Child Tax Credit needs to be balanced with a commitment to increase Child Benefit. We support the idea of Child Benefit and Child Tax Credit as the twin foundations of welfare policy for low-income families. We would not propose to shift resources in a way that would undermine either element. However, we believe that there are good reasons to focus now on increasing Child Benefit rates, thereby rebalancing a system which has become heavily dependent on tax credits as its principal anti-poverty policy. We believe that this would in fact relieve some of the pressure on the tax credit system, allowing the two policies to function more effectively together.

Child Benefit presents negligible disincentives to work, has take up of nearly 100 per cent, is universal and therefore attractive to all families with children, and does not suffer from the complexity and administrative problems associated with Tax Credits. Recent evidence of widespread overpayments and the hardship caused by consequent repayment by low income families has highlighted risks for the recipients of Tax Credits. Along with the complexity of the system, these problems are partly due to the difficulties of marrying weekly benefits with an annual tax system. Child Benefit therefore provides a crucial floor underpinning tax credits, which is not vulnerable to administrative disruptions and which can help tide families over when problems arise with tax credits. It provides a secure and stable form of income, which follows the child through changes in family status, whilst means-tested benefits and tax credits do not do so, because a new claim has to be made when the family unit changes. As well as its role in alleviating poverty – reaching more children living in poverty than any of the benefits and tax credits specifically designed for them – Child Benefit also helps to protect children at times of transition when they are especially vulnerable.[12]

Although the shift from 'benefits' to 'tax credits' has been partly motivated by the desire to end the stigma of 'welfare handouts', our deliberative research suggests that they are still perceived negatively by many of their recipients. While an element of Child Tax Credit is available to households relatively high up the income distribution, they are nonetheless presented as targeting low-income families. They have also become a political target for that reason, with Opposition spokespersons recently attacking the system in a way that does not apply to Child Benefit.

Focusing extra resources through Child Benefit means that all families with children receive the benefit, not just those with low incomes. It is therefore criticised by some as not well targeted. However, it can be argued that Child Benefit is well targeted, in two senses. Firstly, because the rate of child poverty is higher than the rate of adult poverty, it is targeted on poverty; Child Benefit can help prevent poverty, rather than relieving poverty only after the event (as means-tested benefits and tax credits do). Countries with more universal benefits systems (such as in those in Scandinavia) tend to be those which have dealt with child poverty more effectively. This is partly to do with their focus on investment in all children as well as their gender equality perspective. Secondly, Child Benefit is targeted on children and we are concerned with horizontal equity as well as with vertical equity. Families with children are fairly entitled to more support than those without children, even when they have the same incomes. We give additional support to people with disabilities because they have extra costs, and so would have lower living standards on the same level of income. There is a similar argument for Child Benefit, which meets some of the additional costs of having children. Child Benefit also redistributes resources over the individual or family lifecycle, from the times when resources are greater in relation to needs to a time when they are lower in relation to needs.

▶ Recommendation 9
*Overall **benefit rates for children** should increase at least in line with average earnings or faster, so that their standard of living rises and more children are lifted out of poverty. Universal Child Benefit and means-tested Child Tax Credit should remain the twin foundations of this approach, but the system should be re-balanced to give a greater role for **Child Benefit**. This would allow both elements to work more effectively alongside each other. One option would be to*

increase the rate of Child Benefit for second and subsequent children over the medium term, to bring these into line with rates for the first child. One option would be to increase the rate of Child Benefit for second and subsequent children over the medium term so that it is closer to the rate for the first child.

Although the risk of poverty amongst large families has fallen since 1998/9,[13] it remains the case that families with two or more children are less able to meet the cost of their children than one-child families. This holds true even when 'equivalence scales that allow for economies of scale within households' are used.[14] As Adam and Brewer argue, 'changes in the tax and benefits system since 1975 have tended to favour one-child households'.[15] Increasing the lower rates of Child Benefit currently received by second and subsequent children is important, therefore, because it would help close the gap between one-child households and larger families that has grown over time.

Furthermore, we believe that an exclusive focus on improving benefit rates for children will eventually militate against the achievement of equal life chances for all. Reviewing adult rates is a priority because these have lagged behind benefit rates for children and are not allowing recipients to share in improved living standards. Income support rates for adults of working age have now fallen far below the official poverty line: income support is £44.50 per week for a single person aged 18-24, compared with £109.45 in pension credit for a single pensioner. There is no coherent justification for this discrepancy. First, we are not convinced by the argument that this is necessary to maintain employment incentives for this group. Second, we are convinced that very low income levels for parents to be, and especially for pregnant mothers, are seriously detrimental to the life chances of their future children. Third, as a number of children's charities and the Women's Budget Group have argued, adult rates paid at below the poverty line diminish the impact of the welcome improvements that have been made to the children's IS rates. The living standards of children cannot be divorced from those of the parents with whom they live.

The government therefore needs to review the adequacy of rates of adult income support and job seekers' allowance paid to those without and without children. Despite our focus on children, we thus believe that benefit rates for non-working adults should be raised to adequacy levels over the medium term, through the incorporation of minimum income standards into the setting of income support, as proposed by the Committee on Work and Pensions.[16] If this were to prove politically or financially impossible, then it would increase the urgency of reconsidering the benefit rates for pregnant women (see Recommendation 8), given the detrimental impact of poverty to their unborn children.

▶ **Recommendation 10**

*We endorse the priority that the government has given to improving the level of direct financial support for children. However, the present low level of **financial support for adults with and without children not in paid work** threatens to militate against the effectiveness of other policies directed at improving children's life chances. Levels of financial support for this group should therefore be increased to adequacy level as measured by minimum income standards. This would help protect today's children and those yet to be born from the effects of poverty as well as recognise the needs of adults living on benefit.*

3.4.2 Earnings

For most children in the UK, their parents' earnings from employment are the primary source of household income. Earnings are central to both poverty and inequality, and therefore to life chances. The government's central focus has been on increasing employment rates, both in the economy as a whole and among disadvantaged groups such as lone parents, ethnic minorities, people aged over 50, those living in the most deprived areas and disabled people. Treasury and DWP objectives in this area do include specific targets to narrow the gaps between the overall employment rate and the rates for disadvantaged groups. This is one good example of how parts of government are implementing the life chances approach which we want to see adopted coherently across the board.

The government has adopted a 'work first' approach to employment. The central focus of initiatives such as the New Deals and Jobcentre Plus has been on helping people obtain paid work, rather than on building up their human capital. We believe that it should be a key policy priority to develop a better understanding of how to build the capacities of those adults currently facing barriers to employment, and how to improve the chances of retention and progression for those in low-paid work, and welcome recent government moves in this direction.

The National Minimum Wage has improved the incomes of many low paid people. It has also reduced the overall gender pay gap, as many of the beneficiaries were low paid women. The government was careful to introduce the National Minimum Wage at a level and in a way (with an independent Commission overseeing the process) designed both to avoid any harm to employment levels and to reassure business representatives. Predictions that a minimum wage would cost hundred of thousands of jobs and would trigger high inflation have simply been proved wrong. But the minimum wage in the UK is still relatively low in relation to median earnings, and many children live in poverty even with one or more parent in paid work.

In particular, an increased minimum wage would raise the household incomes of significant numbers of lone parents living in poverty who earn the minimum wage. It would also improve incentives to work. Given that women are more often the lower wage earners of two income couples, and that the evidence shows that mothers are more likely to prioritise spending on children, an increased minimum wage will help tackle child poverty in some cases, and will also mean that women are better placed to keep their children out of poverty in the event of relationship break-up. Besides being very important for the government as a public sector employer, increases in the minimum wage also signal that some of the burden of addressing poverty and income inequality belongs to the private sector, and not just to the public finances.[17]

▶ **Recommendation 11**
Many children live in poverty despite one or both parents doing paid work. The **minimum wage** *should be increased relative to average earnings as rapidly as is compatible with continued increases in employment rates for groups with currently low employment rates (including certain ethnic minorities, disabled people and lone parents), and with continued economic stability and growth.*

Despite successfully introducing a minimum wage, the government has shown little concern for broader income inequalities. Wage inequality rose significantly during the 1980s and early 1990s, before levelling out from the mid 1990s onwards.[18] On most summary measures, income inequality has not fallen overall since 1997,[19] though redistributive measures since 1997 have prevented further increases in income inequality which would have occurred had the 1996 tax and benefits system simply been annually uprated.[20] But nor is it the case that overall wage inequality is growing inexorably, although wage inequality remains at a high level.[21] While it is sometimes asserted that those who are interested in achieving a more equal distribution of income are fighting unstoppable labour market forces tending to greater inequality, the evidence does not in fact support this. The issue of wider income inequalities is addressed further in section 3.4.4.

3.4.3 Taxation

The Commission does not take current government spending plans to be an absolute constraint on our recommendations. Abolishing child poverty and addressing unfair inequalities in life chances are both first order objectives, whereas the size of the public sector is only a means to various ends. The balance between state and private is essentially a political choice and not a matter of economic necessity, as different economically successful countries such as the USA, the UK and Sweden demonstrate. However, we recognise that increasing the size of the public sector requires public support for the concomitant increases in taxation. Our recommendations here draw on the Fabian Commission on Taxation and Citizenship, chaired by Professor Raymond Plant, which reported in November 2000, providing an authoritative analysis of the policy and politics of taxation and public spending.

Taxation is the principal source of funds for the public services, benefits and tax credits that are key tools to combat poverty and improve opportunities for disadvantaged children. But it also affects household incomes more immediately. As noted in section 2.6, the lowest income fifth of households with children still pay around a third of their gross income in taxes.[22] Direct taxes on income have a major role in reducing the overall level of inequality in the UK but the overall impact of taxation, including indirect taxes, is slightly regressive and so adds to overall income inequality. The progressive impact of direct taxes on overall inequality depends on patterns of spending, and in practice is outweighed by the stronger regressive impact of the many indirect taxes – principally VAT and various duties.

The key arguments for the introduction of a new higher rate of income tax for top earners, proposed by the Fabian Commission on Taxation and Citizenship, remain: that this would make the tax system more progressive; that it is fair for the highest earners to pay a higher marginal rate than those just over the 40 per cent threshold; and that it would be unlikely to affect work incentives. In addition, the dramatic growth of top incomes described in section 2.6 of this report reinforces the point that it would be fairer for the highest earners to pay a greater share of their income in tax. We recognise that the government has committed itself not to raise the top or basic rate of income tax during the current parliament, repeating the pledges on income tax rates made in 1997 and 2001. We believe that, given Labour's ambitions on child poverty, the party should avoid making a similar pledge at the next election.

Inheritance Tax has not been significantly reformed since 1997. The current system has numerous flaws. It is relatively easy to avoid, especially for the very wealthy who have access to good advice about avoidance mechanisms and can afford to give away the bulk of their assets more than seven years before death. The current system can more accurately be described as an Estates Tax. A £500,000 estate is currently taxed in the same way whether it is bequeathed to a single individual or divided between 50 people, taking no account of the financial circumstances of the recipient. So there is no fiscal incentive for people to disperse their wealth, while the inheritance is affected by tax in the same way regardless of whether the inheritor is wealthy or poor

This case was outlined by the Fabian Commission on Taxation and Citizenship and developed further in the Fabian report *Wealth's Fair Measure*. The model proposed was a capital receipts tax levied on the cumulative total of both gifts and legacies received by donees, which would provide incentives for capital dispersion and close the key avoidance loophole of lifetime gifts. While this would require records to be kept of all major capital receipts, it is a model which operates successfully in other countries, such as Ireland.[23]

Implementing a life chances agenda will have an impact on the balance of government spending and on raising revenues through taxation. We need a taxation regime that raises the necessary public funds and we are also interested in income tax rate reforms that would reduce the burden on people on low incomes and reduce the overall level of income inequality.

▶ **Recommendation 12**

*The UK **tax system** currently takes a similar share of income across the income distribution, and should become more progressive. We support the recommendations of the previous Fabian Commission on Taxation and Citizenship for the introduction of a new higher rate of income tax for top earners, and a reform of inheritance tax to shift the burden of such taxation from the estate of the deceased to the recipients of bequests.*

The political ability to drop the tax pledge and, even more so, the public legitimacy of any new top rate for the highest earners must primarily depend on winning a public argument for the use of additional revenues. This was the case with the government's 2002 decision to increase National Insurance contributions by 1p in the pound to put £8 billion extra into the National Health Service, which proved to be the most popular of Labour's post-1997 budgets. We believe that the additional revenue from a new top rate of income tax should be directed to improving public services for disadvantaged children, and to increasing direct financial support to address poverty. As such, it should be publicly promoted as designed to improve the life chances of disadvantaged children.[24]

Lower-income households pay a higher share of their income than better-off households in Council Tax, despite the existence of council tax benefit. At present the most valuable properties are charged three times the rate of the least valuable ones, and the current distribution of land and property taxation reflects 1991 property values. Since then, property prices have grown far more in the most economically successful areas, especially London and the South East. The simplest way to achieve a progressive shift would be to re-value all properties and introduce new valuation bands at the top and bottom of the Council Tax system, with a wider spread of rates between the most and least expensive properties. We do not underestimate the political difficulties of such a move, demonstrated by the government's postponement of the planned 2007 domestic property revaluation. But we are concerned that this debate is dominated at the moment by the voices and interests of the more affluent (particularly in London and the greater south east of England) to the exclusion of larger numbers of lower income households in less economically successful areas who suffer real losses under the current system and would be the 'winners' from such a reform. We believe that two principles should guide any reform: firstly that the new system must more accurately reflect the distribution of wealth than it does at present; and secondly that the new system should be regularly updated so that the burden of land and property tax and the pattern of housing wealth never again get so badly out of alignment as they have done since 1991.

3.4.4 Narrowing inequalities of income and wealth

Public policy has a powerful impact on household incomes in many ways. Public services such as education and health affect our ability to secure employment and earn an income; economic policy affects employment and incomes, and taxes, benefits and public services redistribute income between different households. But that is not the only role that politics and government play. Political leadership can also play an important role in influencing the social norms and the broader public climate which helps to determine wages and the distribution of income, though these are also affected by other actors and broader public attitudes. While income inequalities after taxes and benefits are the better indicator of living standards and spending power, it is also important to address inequalities in earnings before taxes and benefits for two reasons: first, because this reduces the redistributional 'workload' for the tax and benefit system; and second, because the rewards people receive from work represent recognition of the value society places upon their contribution.

The case for ending low pay and for working towards a more equal wages structure is supported by evidence from Sweden, Denmark, Norway and to a lesser extent Holland and Austria: all countries with strong economies, high employment levels and more equal pay. As a result, people's lives are less socially stratified. A doctor, a hospital clerk and a hospital cleaner in Nordic countries are more likely to live in the same neighbourhood and send their children to the same day care nurseries and the same schools and afford similar holidays and cars.

We do not suggest that gross inequalities in pay, status and conditions can be ended overnight. Change can only occur gradually, as indeed it did in these countries over many social democratic decades. The key issue is to achieve broad political commitment to the desired direction of travel for an agreed purpose – the eradication of child poverty and more equal life chances for all.

As stressed through the report, we are principally concerned about income inequality because of its effect on the life chances of children in lower income families. However, income inequalities have effects throughout society. Part Two of this report repeatedly shows people in the *middle* of the earnings distribution doing systematically worse across a range of life chances dimensions, than people at the top, just as people at the bottom do systematically worse than people in the middle. Moreover, research suggests that the overall quality of social relations in a society is directly and adversely affected by wide inequalities. Income inequalities are not just a matter of concern for people living in poverty. So we are in favour of a narrower gap between high incomes and moderate incomes, as well as between moderate and low incomes. We are not just concerned with the mobility of people between different positions, but also with reducing the distance between 'good' and 'bad' outcomes, so that social position becomes less important and society becomes less stratified.

Wealth is fundamental to life chances and is even more unevenly distributed than income. The 1980s did not see an explosion in wealth inequality to parallel that of income inequality but by the 1990s the widening gap in disposable income was feeding through into growing wealth inequalities. The share of wealth held by the top 1 per cent rose from 17 per cent to 24 per cent from 1991 to 2002, and that of the top 10 per cent from 47 per cent to 66 per cent.[25] Meanwhile a third of the population have little or no accessible savings. Possessing modest amounts of wealth can be an important protective 'buffer' for low income families, allowing them to deal with unexpected events and costs. Large concentrations of wealth allow families to transmit advantages in life chances to their children via privileged access to housing, education, and opportunities to take risks such as starting a business. A society where more and less affluent families do not live in the same areas, use the same public services, or share common risks and interests as part of a community of citizens is bad for social cohesion and quality of life.

The government has taken important steps since 1997 to establish asset based welfare as a new element of the welfare state, particularly via the Child Trust Fund and the Savings Gateway. These policies focused on the 'asset poor' and are to be welcomed as an addition to policies designed to tackle low incomes.

But there has been little focus or progress in relation to asset inequality. As our vision is of a more equal society, rather than simply one where the most disadvantaged children have better outcomes than at present, we believe it is important that public policy both builds up the assets of those with low income and small savings, and that it works against the continuing polarisation of wealth.

We therefore recommend that the government, in addition to making an explicit commitment to increasing the minimum wage, should develop and monitor indicators of income inequality (before and after taxes and benefits) and wealth inequality, and adopt the objective of reducing income and wealth inequalities over time, in recognition of their impact on life chances.[26] However, we do not think it makes sense to set a numerical target at this stage, before the general principle has been accepted and further work has been done on the most appropriate measure to adopt.

▶ **Recommendation 13**
We believe that the government should set a target to reduce **income and wealth inequalities** *over time where these affect life chances, and should develop and then give prominence to monitoring appropriate indicators of income and wealth inequality.*

▶ **Recommendation 14**
The government should convene a **Royal Commission on the Distribution of Income and Wealth**, *whose remit should include reviewing the impact of existing patterns of remuneration and wealth on children's life chances, engaging the public with its deliberations and making proposals focused on improving the life chances of disadvantaged children.*

Conclusions

Conclusions

Since 1997 the Labour government has made some impressive commitments to addressing disadvantage and improving public services, including its pledge to abolish child poverty in the UK by 2020. There has been real, measured progress on a number of fronts. Child poverty has fallen and standards have risen in many areas of the core public services. These achievements have been combined with sound public finances and a strong economy. The commitment to tackling discrimination in all its forms has been reflected in the passage of the Human Rights Act of 1998. This is an impressive record on which to build.

However, we are faced with three major, pressing challenges. Firstly, the number of children in poverty in the UK remains high, with some 2.6 million children still living in households below the poverty line[27]. The 2020 target, and the interim goal of reducing child poverty by half by 2010 relative to its 1999 baseline, both look difficult to achieve and require significant new political momentum.

Secondly, life chances remain very unequal. Children from disadvantaged backgrounds have much worse chances in terms of their infant mortality rates; their subsequent cognitive and physical development; their experience of childhood; their outcomes at school; and later access to higher education and jobs. In many cases these inequalities are just as wide now as they were in 1997, and in some cases they are widening. Where children are born and who their parents are is still central to their chances in life to an extent that should offend against our basic instincts for fairness.

Thirdly, despite a sound underlying basis of support for redistributive policies[28], the public does not currently give high priority to tackling poverty and inequality. Public attitudes towards people living in poverty are dominated by stereotypes, mistrust and a lack of empathy. Support for some of the government's existing ambitions is thus thin, and a more ambitious agenda would be even more demanding.

The progressive movement in the UK can and must rise to these challenges. Addressing child poverty must continue to be a high priority, and we should resist the temptation to play down the importance of family income just because other factors are also important for children's life chances. In addition we must give new emphasis to improving the life chances of children from disadvantaged backgrounds and especially to closing the gap between their experiences and those of their more fortunate peers. Finally, we must grasp the challenge of building broader, deeper public support for these goals than exists at the moment. All of this must be done in a way that is politically sustainable in the long term.

We believe that the life chances framework has a major role to play in meeting these challenges. Firstly, it helps to clarify the purposes of a progressive movement, cutting through stale debates about equality of opportunity vs. equality of outcome. The life chances framework says that both matter: we want more equal opportunities for children from different backgrounds to have good outcomes throughout their lives. In particular the life chances framework clarifies how equality of opportunity is impossible in the context of wide inequalities of income and wealth which hold some children back and privilege others.

Secondly, it provides a framework for understanding how life chances are affected by a wide range of factors, and thus helps us to design specific objectives and policies. It makes us realise there is no 'magic bullet' for tackling inequality, and instead draws attention to the impact of a range of family and parental factors, a child's physical, social and economic environment, and the role of public services. It also focuses our minds on the really key inequalities – in child health, development and education in particular because of their profound impact on later life – and also on the importance of all children enjoying a flourishing childhood. As well as helping policy makers in this way, the life chances framework should help organisations such as public bodies be clear about their own objectives and the role they play in improving life chances.

Thirdly, we believe that the life chances framework can help us develop a compelling public narrative about this. If the government is successful with its anti-poverty strategy then the number of children living in poverty will steadily shrink, becoming a less and less politically significant group. However, people will always want the best possible life chances – not just those people at the bottom but those in the middle too. A life chances approach could help build a broader and more durable political coalition for tackling disadvantage. This should sit alongside a strategy for combating negative stereotypes and increasing public understanding of the way in which poverty harms life chances. Although our focus in this report has been domestic, the life chances framework should also form part of a consistent and principled approach to economic and social rights at the international level, which would tackle poverty in both industrialised and developing countries in a co-ordinated way.

One of our over-arching conclusions is that politicians and policy makers should put life chances at the centre of what they do. For a minister in a progressive government, every policy should be tested against the questions: 'What does this do for life chances? What does it do for those who currently have the worst chances in life? Does it reduce or widen inequalities in life chances?' For those delivering public services, for example in local government, the NHS, the police, or the voluntary sector, the same questions should apply. Those of us – including the general public – who want to hold politicians and public bodies to account should get used to measuring them against these three tests.

The policy recommendations that flow from our work attempt to address some of the most pressing issues for children who currently have poor life chances. It is far from being a complete list, and all of the recommendations would require more detailed work before they could be implemented. In particular we have not attempted to put a price tag on our proposals. Aside from the technical difficulties of doing so, we want to avoid getting side-tracked into a debate about costs and tax rates and instead focus on the objectives of policy, the most promising options for further investigation, and the ways to build political support for the long term project of tackling poor life chances in the UK.

There is a lot we do not know about exactly why children from some backgrounds have systematically worse chances than others, and there certainly needs to be more empirical work done on understanding these issues. But if we wait for certainty we will wait for ever, and the problem is too important and too urgent for that. In the meantime we must work on the basis of a convincing analysis that fits with the evidence we do have. We have tried to set out such a story in Part Two of this report.

Public services matter for life chances, and income matters too. Child poverty is important because it blights life chances, including the chance to live a happy childhood. Whilst we welcome the government's work to date on child poverty, we want to see the issue moving up the agenda and for eradicating child poverty to be one of the key strategic challenges addressed by the 2007 Comprehensive Spending Review (Recommendation 1).

The government's anti-poverty strategy has focused very strongly on increasing employment rates. We recognise that this is central, and support the government's commitment to increasing employment rates among disadvantaged groups such as ethnic minorities, disabled people and lone parents. However, direct financial support is also important – benefits and tax credits play a central role in reducing poverty at the moment and are likely to remain central for the foreseeable future.

If the government is to have any hope of achieving its poverty targets, it must consistently up-rate benefits for families with children at least in line with the rate of growth in average earning. Whilst universal Child Benefit and the means-tested Child Tax Credit should remain the twin pillars of income support for families with children, there should be a re-balancing of the system towards Child Benefit. One option would be to increase the rate of Child Benefit for second and subsequent children over the medium term so that it is closer to the rate for the first child. This would take some of the pressure off the Tax Credits system as well as achieving higher take up rates and wider public buy-in (Recommendation 9).

We also believe that there needs to be more focus on low income among adults not in work. Poverty among low income parents impacts directly on the life chances of their children; poverty among childless adults without work, particularly pregnant women, can affect the life-chances of future children. As a first step towards additional financial support, higher rates of benefits should be made payable during pregnancy, to help address poverty among pregnant women and to promote the health of babies even before birth. Our preferred long-term solution would be to increase adult rates of Income Support to adequacy levels, as measured by minimum income standards. (Recommendation 8, Recommendation 10.)

It will always be difficult to close the gap in life chances whilst there are large inequalities in household income and wealth, and a number of our recommendations address this issue. We therefore recommend that the government should give more prominence to monitoring indicators of income inequality, before and after taxes and benefits, and set a target to reduce income inequalities over time. Echoing the conclusions of the Fabian Tax Commission, we want to see the tax system become more progressive, we support the principle of a higher top rate of income tax on the highest earners, and recommend a reform of Inheritance Tax to shift its burden from estates to recipients. We also support a rising Minimum Wage to bring up relative earnings at the other end of the income spectrum. In addition we recommend an official review of the overall distribution of income and wealth with a focus on the impact of inequalities in income and wealth on children's life chances. (Recommendation 11, Recommendation 12, Recommendation 13, Recommendation 14.)

Turning to the life course, another overarching conclusion is that government should measure the inequalities in life chances between different groups, should regularly report on them, and should adopt explicit objectives to narrow them. (Recommendation 2) Our main conclusions for the life course form a relatively simple narrative. The government must hold its nerve on the early years agenda, extend its focus to the period before birth, and address educational inequalities at school.

A broad range of international evidence, allied to an impressive body of theoretical work, suggests that good quality childcare services can make a great difference to children's life chances in the period between birth and the start of formal schooling. The major investment made in Sure Start and the subsequent Children's Centres needs to be sustained and extended. Whilst the design of these services should evolve on the basis of the best evidence, the principle that the state has the central role in funding the services and ensuring the availability of high quality provision must be defended. High quality childcare, focused on improving child development but also facilitating parental employment, should become a permanent feature of the modern welfare state, and this is likely to require significant additional public resources as coverage and quality are improved. Whilst government will continue to play a role in subsidising parental demand for childcare, we believe that public spending should be re-balanced towards directly supporting the supply of high quality places (Recommendation 5).

In addition more attention needs to be focused on the period before birth, where some of the most damaging problems are created by maternal poverty, stress, poor nutrition and harmful health behaviours. The existing social class gap in infant mortality and birthweight, where women from routine or manual occupational backgrounds are 50 per cent more likely to have an infant die in their first year than professional women, is a national disgrace. One part of the solution, as already mentioned, will be to improve the income of pregnant women via benefit reforms, and another will be to refocus existing maternity services on those groups of women from low income and low socio-economic status backgrounds who are known to be at high risk. (Recommendation 3, Recommendation 4.)

Our central recommendation for the school years is the development of explicit targets to reduce inequalities in educational attainment between disadvantaged groups and their peers from Foundation Stage onwards. This should happen in time for their inclusion in the Department for Education and Skills' revised Public Service Agreements in Comprehensive Spending Review 2007. The government deserves credit for policies which have driven up standards at the worst performing schools, but floor targets have not narrowed the gaps in pupil attainment. Gap targets do not have to mean 'levelling down' and already exist in relation to key health and employment objectives.

By the same token, school policies are needed which explicitly address inequalities in life chances, especially in the area of admissions, funding and the school audit and inspection system. Taking educational inequality at school seriously would be an iconic move for the Labour Party, and one which would set a clear dividing line between them and their political opponents. (Recommendation 6, Recommendation 7.) We also urge the government to do more to ensure that every child is able to participate fully in school life. In particular, more needs to be done to help parents meet the extra costs of education, such as activities, equipment and uniform, and so alleviate the stress and stigma that lack of resources can mean for parents and children alike.

Public attitudes towards poverty and inequality, and to the policies necessary to address these problems, present us with a puzzle. On the one hand we know that large majorities of the public think that the gap between high and low incomes is too big, and that there is broad underlying support for a redistributive welfare system and public services. On the other hand we know that poverty and disadvantage are not high on the public agenda, and that people are nervous about the state acting in an explicitly redistributive manner to reduce inequalities.

The recent 'Make Poverty History' campaign has much to teach us about campaigning against domestic poverty. Its central message is one of optimism – about people's capacity to respond to an essentially moral argument – which must be tempered with the realisation that poverty in the UK is not usually so stark as the absolute destitution experienced by the starving African child. If we want to end child poverty at home then we will have to build the same kind of public support.

We believe that part of the solution to this puzzle can be found in our deliberative work, which shows that attitudes towards people living in poverty are dominated by stereotypes, mistrust and a lack of understanding. What is needed is not sympathy, but rather a revolution in empathy: greater public understanding of the true nature of poverty and disadvantage, the way it affects daily life, and how it damages children's life chances. Everyone who cares about these issues should be giving a high priority to publicising realistic narratives about disadvantage and combating unrealistic stereotypes of the 'undeserving poor'. The government has a key role to play in this, leading by example in their public discussion about poverty and disadvantage. Government must also be careful to avoid undermining public support and inadvertently reinforcing stereotypes.

We believe that it is possible to make an ambitious case for ending child poverty and narrowing inequalities in life chances. Attitudes to unequal life chances are complex. Our deliberative research suggests that people can easily blame parents for their own poverty, but that they do understand some of the ways in which unequal parental resources generate unequal life chances for children. They also understand the need for public policy to support families for the good of their children. There is an opportunity here to work with the grain of public opinion, using realistic stories about life chances to make a progressive political case.

Our deliberative research suggests that once the public understand that poverty exists in the UK and that it has a real impact on the lives of those who live with it, they see it as wasteful and unnecessary in our affluent society. They recognise the powerful 'business case' for tackling poverty and disadvantage alongside the moral arguments. Once they know about the 2020 target to abolish poverty in the UK, and understand that real progress has already been made, they support the long term goal. But far too few people do appear to know about it, which reinforces the case we make for moving it up the agenda.

Equalising life chances and ending child poverty should sit together at the heart of a progressive vision of what makes a fair society in which all can flourish. We believe that this vision can have real public appeal. It is a challenge to us all: to improve children's life chances, to narrow the gap in life chances, and to make poverty history at home.

Notes

1 The Social Exclusion Unit's *Report on Teenage Pregnancy*, published in June 1999, set out two national targets: to halve the under 18 conception rate by 2010 (and establish a firm downward trend in the under 16 rate); and to increase the participation of teenage parents in education, training or work, to reduce their risk of long-term social exclusion.

In June 2002 Hazel Blears announced a target to reduce the risk of long-term social exclusion by increasing the participation of teenage parents aged 16 to 19 in employment, education or training to 60 per cent by 2010.

2 Paul Nicholson (2005): personal communication.

3 Pregnant women who smoke are more likely to miscarry, or to have pre-term deliveries and low birth weight babies, while their babies are more likely to die of sudden infant death, or to suffer from respiratory problems such as chest infections and asthma (DH 1998).

4 The Work and Families Bill, introduced into Parliament in October 2005, contains provision for fathers to take up to six months' unpaid leave, and to receive paternity pay for up to three months if a mother returns to work after six months and before her maternity leave ends.

5 Equal Opportunities Commission 2005.

6 The National Audit Office 2004.

7 Waldfogel 2004; Alakeson 2005.

8 Kelly 2005.

9 Department for Education and Skills 2005.

10 Barnados *et al.* 2005.

11 Mayo 2005.

12 Adelman *et al.* 2003.

13 The latest HBAI figures describe the risk of poverty for larger families as having 'decreased markedly' over time. See DWP 2005.

14 Adam and Brewer 2004, p. 56.

15 *Ibid.*

16 Committee on Work and Pensions 2004.

17 We recognise that the impact of an increased minimum wage on official child poverty figures will be less than intuition may suggest. As many minimum wage earners are in households with more than median total income, raising the minimum wage would also raise the official 'poverty line' of 60 per cent of median income. This is not an argument against an increased minimum wage: it would be better treated as a warning of the limitations of seeing poverty from a snapshot, household based perspective, rather than a dynamic, individually based one and as a message that anti-poverty strategies need to be more than a 'one club' policy.

18 See Robinson 2005.

19 As discussed in Part Three, income inequality is driven by the widening divide between the bottom 10 per cent and top 10 per cent, while the incomes of the middle 80 have in fact become more equal. See Hills 2004.

20 Brewer *et al.* 2004.

21 See Atkinson 1999.

22 Jones 2005.

23 Le Grand and Nissan 2000.

24 The Fabian Commission on Taxation and Citizenship restricted itself to taxation proposals, so this is a different proposal for the use of the revenue than that made by the Commission in 2000, which suggested that it should be used to increase the personal allowance, taking more lower-income individuals out of income tax; or in addition to increase the 40 per cent rate threshold.

25 HM Revenue & Customs 2004.

26 In fact, some indicators of income inequality already exist, but are not being made use of: under the National Action Plans on Social Inclusion set by the EU, member states have a duty to monitor the relationship between the income of the bottom 20 per cent and the top 20 per cent. Greater use could be made of this, and other indicators of income inequality.

27 As before, these figures are for 2003/04 and are based on a relative poverty measure (60per cent of median equivalised contemporary household income) before housing costs. Using a relative poverty measure after housing costs, 3.5 million children were living in poverty in 2003/04.

28 See for example, *British Social Attitudes Survey 22nd Report*, 2005/06 edition.

Appendices

Appendix A

Members of the Commission

Chair: Lord Victor Adebowale CBE
Chief Executive of Turning Point.

Lord Victor Adebowale is an independent peer and Chief Executive of Turning Point, the UK's leading social care organisation, which has more than 200 services nationwide. Turning Point works with people facing a range of complex needs including substance misuse, mental health problems and learning disabilities. Previously he worked for Patchwork Community Housing Association and was Regional Director of the Ujima Housing Association, Britain's largest Black-led housing association. Before joining Turning Point, he was Director of the Alcohol Recovery Project and most recently Chief Executive of the leading youth homelessness charity Centrepoint.

Fran Bennett
Senior Research Fellow at the Department of Social Policy and Social Work, University of Oxford and freelance consultant on social policy issues.

Fran Bennett currently works half time as a senior research fellow at the Department of Social Policy and Social Work, University of Oxford and half time as a self-employed social policy researcher/consultant. She works in particular on poverty and social security, and is also interested in gender issues. She has previously worked as deputy director and then director of the Child Poverty Action Group, and as a policy advisor on UK and European poverty issues for Oxfam. She is currently working with Prof Jonathan Bradshaw as a UK non-government expert on the National Action Plan for Social Inclusion.

Ruth Cadbury

Chair-Elect of the Barrow Cadbury Trust and an Executive Councillor in the London Borough of Hounslow.

Ruth Cadbury is Chair-Elect of the Barrow Cadbury Trust. She is a Councillor and Lead Executive member for Children and Life-long Learning, in the London Borough of Hounslow. Ruth has a professional background in Town Planning and Community Development.

Richard Exell OBE

Senior Policy Officer at the TUC.

Richard writes briefings and reports on labour market and social security issues, and is responsible for co-ordinating the TUC's network of Unemployed Workers' Centres. Richard is a member of the European TUC's working party on social protection, and was a member of the trade union team in the discussions that eventually produced the European Directive on parental leave. Richard is a member of the Social Security Advisory Committee and the Disability Rights Commission. He is 49 years old and is married with a daughter, Madeleine, aged 12.

Ruth Lister CBE AcSS

Professor of Social Policy, Loughborough University and Donald Dewar Visiting Professor of Social Justice, Glasgow University (2005-2006).

Ruth Lister is a former Director of the Child Poverty Action Group. She has served on a number of commissions, including the Commission on Social Justice and the Commission on Poverty, Participation and Power, and is a trustee of the Community Development Foundation. She has published widely in the areas of poverty, citizenship, gender and welfare reform. Her latest book is *Poverty* (2004).

David Piachaud
Professor of Social Policy at the London School of Economics.

David Piachaud is Professor of Social Policy at the London School of Economics and an Associate of the Centre for Analysis of Social Exclusion. He was Social Policy Adviser in the Prime Minister's Policy Unit (1974-79) and has been Consultant to the European Commission, ILO, OECD and WHO. He has written papers and books on children, poverty, social security, social exclusion and social policy; for the Fabian Society he wrote *What's Wrong with Fabianism?*

Aftab Rahman
Community Cohesion Co-ordinator at the Government Office for the West Midlands.

Aftab Rahman joined Government Office West Midlands as the Community Cohesion Co-ordinater in December 2001 with responsibilities for promoting community cohesion in collaboration with both the statutory and voluntary sectors. Previously he worked for the Bangladeshi Youth Forum as the Development Manager and for Worcester City Council as a Youth Development Worker, where he was responsible for engaging and involving young people in decision-making processes. He has contributed to the development of a number of successful community organisations; and he currently sits on several committees and management boards, including Pioneers leading the way, The Drum, Asian Resource Centre and Shapla Football League.

Andrew Robinson MBE
Head of Community Development Banking at Nat West and Royal Bank of Scotland.

Andrew Robinson leads a cross-RBS group team responsible for re-thinking the provision of financial services for sectors that have not been well served by the UK banking industry. The current emphasis of his work are the 1,997 'most disadvantaged' wards in the UK. He is a director of a number of organisations promoting community-based, community-led solutions to encouraging enterprise, tackling poverty and reforming local public service delivery. He is also trustee of the Community Development Foundation, a non departmental public body of the Home Office; a member of the ODPM's working group on the Community Ownership and Management of Assets; a member of the DTI/Small Business Services strategy implementation working group on Social Enterprise; and SEEDA's Inclusion committee. He has a MBA, is a graduate of Common Purpose and a Fellow of the RSA.

Peter Townsend AcSS FBA
Centennial Professor of International Social Policy at the London School of Economics

Peter Townsend is Centennial Professor of International Social Policy at the London School of Economics, where he continues to teach postgraduate students about human rights, development and social policy. In 1963 he was appointed Professor of Sociology at the University of Essex upon its foundation and in 1982 moved to the University of Bristol, where he is now also Emeritus Professor. He has worked lately with UNICEF, and was consultant to the UN at the time of the World Summit for Social Development at Copenhagen in 1995. He helped to found the Child Poverty Action Group in 1965 and the Disability Alliance in 1973, was Chair of both organisations for 20 years and continues to be President of both. He is Vice-President of the Fabian Society. His latest book is *Inequalities of Health: The Welsh Dimension* (2005).

Polly Toynbee
Political and social commentator for the Guardian

Polly Toynbee is a political and social commentator for the Guardian newspaper. Previously she was the BBC's Social Affairs Editor. She has written books on the NHS, adoption and work. Her most recent books include *Better or Worse? Has Labour*

Delivered? (with David Walker) and *Hard Work: Life in Low-Pay Britain*. She has won the George Orwell Prize, and Columnist of the Year in the National Press Awards. She is President of the Social Policy Association. She has four children and lives in Lambeth, London.

Secretariat to the Commission:
Louise Bamfield, Richard Brooks and Sadia Haider.

Louise Bamfield
Research Fellow at the Fabian Society.

Louise Bamfield was formerly a doctoral student at Pembroke College, University of Cambridge where she completed a PhD in the philosophy of education, focusing on citizenship education and the communitarian critique of John Rawls's political liberalism. She is currently working at the Fabian Society on poverty and educational inequalities, looking at the consequences of poverty for children's educational and subsequent life chances.

Richard Brooks
Research Director at the Fabian Society.

Before joining the Fabian Society Richard Brooks worked at the Institute for Public Policy Research, the Prime Minister's Strategy Unit, and the Labour Party Policy Unit on a wide range of public policy issues including: pensions and welfare reform; industrial and business policy; local government finance and structure; public private partnerships; and public service delivery. He is also a Labour councillor and the cabinet member for resources in the London Borough Tower Hamlets.

Appendix B

The Commission's terms of reference

The Commission was launched in March 2004. Its terms of reference were:

"The Commission's aim was to make a major contribution to the future development of the government's strategy to end child poverty and to reframe the public debate on this issue.

Using a 'life chances' framework, the research considered both practical policy solutions to child poverty, and the more theoretical underpinnings of the strategy. The focus was on some or all of the following: income and occupation, health and well-being, education, environmental quality, security and safety, aspirations, and the ability to make decisions about one's own life in relation to social position. An important part of the project will be to explore the experiences and views of families with experience of poverty themselves.

The Commission will address specifically:

- *Ways of conceptualising child poverty within a life chances framework: what do poverty, equality and mobility mean in contemporary Britain?*

- *The character and performance of existing anti-poverty interventions: is the government's strategy appropriate for the challenge?*

- *The experience of other countries in addressing child poverty: are there lessons to be learned from taking an international perspective?*

- *Ways in which the stated aim of ending child poverty can best be achieved: what more needs to be done to meet the Prime Minister's ambitious target?"*

Appendix C

Research methodology

Deliberative research

For the Fabian Commission on Life Chances and Child Poverty, MORI conducted two group discussions, a three hour extended focus group and a full day workshop on 2nd and 6th February 2005 respectively. The focus group comprised nine people and lasted three hours whilst the workshop comprised 21 participants and lasted six hours.

In both discussions, a representative sample was recruited on the basis of gender, BME status, and age/lifestage within the range 25-45 years (focus group) and 25-65 years (workshop). All participants were drawn from socio-economic classes BC1C2, and participants' professional sectors included teaching, insurance, social work, banking, and leisure. Participants were also screened on the basis of party political affiliation, newspaper readership and the level of priority they attached to the issue of child poverty in Britain.

The objective here was to exclude people who were identifiable as strongly on the left or right of the political spectrum. For practical reasons, however, all were recruited from London and the South East of England. They should not be taken as a representative sample of UK citizens, therefore; but the results of the deliberative research can nonetheless give us useful pointers towards directions for the debate on child poverty and life chances which may chime more or less well with the concerns of people 'in the middle' of the political landscape.

Qualitative research

This small-scale qualitative research project consisted of focus group interviews with members of six grassroots organisations based in London and the West Midlands. The organisations that kindly participated in our focus group research were:

- The Allenscroft Project, Birmingham;

- ATD Fourth World;

- Birmingham Women's Advice and Information Centre, Birmingham;

- Single Parent Action Network, Bristol;

- The Welsh House Farm Project, Birmingham;

- Windows for Sudan, Birmingham.

The focus group discussions explored a range of issues and problems encountered by people in poverty as the 'end-users' of public services, as well as examining the role of local community groups and organisations in helping them to overcome the problems associated with life in poverty. Each focus group lasted for around an hour and a half to two hours, and was led by a moderator using a discussion guide of topics and questions. The research was conducted in summer 2005.